GUARDIAN UNIVERSE

THE GOSPEL IN UNEXPECTED TERMS

GEOFFREY YOUNG

CMD R
PUBLISHING

CMDR Publishing

4025 Postal Way
#50894
Myrtle Beach, SC, 29579
www.cmdrpublishing.com

Revised 14 September 2021.

About the Author.

Geoffrey Young is a Television Producer, Director and Writer of factual and historical programming for Australian and US audiences. He lives in Sydney with his wife and son.

Editorial guidance by Joel Cutter. Proofing by Anne Polley and Joel Cutter. Cover artwork by Faith Oxley and Geoffrey Young. Other contributions by Robert Young, Tommy McCarthy, Louise Edmonds and Joshua Walker. The first printed copy purchased by Alfred de Gouveia.

Cataloguing in Publication Data:

Names: Young, Geoffrey.

Title: The Guardian Universe / by Geoffrey Young.

Description: CMDR Publishing trade paperback edition | Summary: The Christian Gospel message told in terms of the natural and the supernatural.

Identifiers: ISBN 978-1-7355876-4-6 (paperback)

Subjects: Religion. | Spirituality. | Christianity. | Gospel. | Jesus Christ.

CONTENTS

PART I
PROLOGUE

WELCOME TO A WORLD YOU
THINK YOU KNOW

H ave you ever wondered about the unseen? The hidden, the invisible, and the concealed have always held my fascination. In fact, it's something of a passion for me, seeing that which is just out of sight. I don't want to just believe in the supernatural, I want to understand how it works.

I do not care for the spooky or the superstitious, but rather the reality behind the scenes that makes our visible world work. The realm just beyond our own in which lie the answers to love, to hate, to faith, belief and hope. The cogs that drive the inexplicable, the power sources from which the impossible becomes possible. Perhaps, to you, what I'm describing is the supernatural, but I think it to be more *natural* than *super*. I think it's organic like a forest, alive like the trees, and as natural as the wind that moves through the branches.

I believe it's real, complex and intricate. And understanding it is not just possible, but essential.

If you are a Christian as am I, then being constantly

mindful of the unseen is not an optional extra. It may surprise you to discover it is a command.

> Since you have been raised to new life with Christ, set your sights on the realities of heaven, where Christ sits in the place of honor at God's right hand. Think about the things of heaven, not the things of earth.

— COLOSSIANS 3:1-2 NLT

If you have divine life within you, then your mind must pivot to the divine. If your hope is in an unseen reality, then the nature of this reality really must become your business. I am convinced it is mandatory. To fulfil your destiny *requires* it.

> So we don't look at the troubles we can see now; rather, we fix our gaze on things that cannot be seen. For the things we see now will soon be gone, but the things we cannot see will last forever.

— 2 CORINTHIANS 4:18 NLT

It really is a good thing you've picked up this book!

I'm setting out to explain, in simple terms, how the unseen and the seen work together. I'm going to describe a reality that exists all around you, a reality I call the Guardian Universe.

The Guardian Universe is our world, one where the natural and supernatural exist intermingled, side by side. Far from a trivial fascination for the superstitious, understanding the story that is unfolding on both sides of the mortal and immortal hemisphere provides profound answers to some of life's most difficult questions.

Why do bad things happen to good people?

Why does God let evil exist?

If he is all-powerful why does he allow the devil to roam the earth?

And so on.

God never intended us to get by in life with simplistic platitudes like 'God only knows' and 'we'll find out in heaven.' God wants you to know. He wants you not just to seek answers, but he wants to open the door for you to find them.

This book is, as you will discover, not just a journey into the supernatural, but the expansive and extraordinary story of God. It is the story of his Son. It is the Gospel of Jesus Christ, perhaps in terms you've never considered. My fascination is not with angels, nor the Guardians who lend their name to this book. Not at all. My attraction is to you and to me, sons and daughters once lost but now with a pathway by which to be found.

Having said all of that, for a good many of you, I think this will all be *a bit too much*. So you might like to treat this then, as a work of fiction, and you'd be very welcome to do so. It's somewhat less confronting to consider things from an oblique perspective, and to some degree, that's why I begin the book speaking of angels and demons. In today's society, where only what can be seen is real, they have become mere myth. They are, for all intents and purposes, an excellent starting point by which you can find your way into my 'fictional world.'

By the end, however, despite initial misgivings, you may well find that this story is indeed your story. That you are a son or daughter, but of lost and forgotten royal origin. I hope that's the case. If not, I guarantee I will not bore you on the journey – this is not a pathway you've walked before.

As you read this book you'll find that I've included tons of scripture. Bible verses in vast quantities. In some cases, specific verses reappear again and again. I would encourage you - read them. Meditate on them. Consume them as if your life depends on them.

> They are not just idle words for you - they are your life. By them you will live long in the land ...
>
> — DEUTERONOMY 32:47 NIV

If my own words have any value, it will only be to help you ingest the word of God in perfect and pure form: from God's own Spirit directly into your heart. I will have succeeded only in those cases where you can hear God, perhaps for the first time, for yourself. To this end – do not skip a single word of scripture. Dwell on them, consume them, drink them in.

The reality is that in the pages of this book I describe to you a universe that I cannot see, except in my mind's eye. The only truths in this book are the verses of scripture within its pages. The rest, everything I have written, should be understood as no more than a metaphor, perhaps a parable or a hand-drawn map sketched on paper. Their *only* value is in their ability to help you see the words of God in effect right now, in the world around you.

YOUR JOURNEY

S o where does it begin?

The shocking reality that confronts us at the outset is simply this. You and I in the global west are not what we should be.

To peel back our perfectly presented selves, to strip away the well managed and manicured facade reveals our spirit – and I fear when we do, what we discover is shocking to the core. Impoverished, anemic, diseased, pitiful, poor and naked. And the worst of it? We are, for the most part, entirely unaware. We don't even know it.

We look good in this world - but none of that matters. What we are in this world is passing away.

By the end of this book I will have prosecuted the case that this is not what was intended. We were created to be warriors. Nobility, masters, leaders. Each a weapon in God's hand. But how many of us measure up to this calling?

Rather than a warrior, we're on the couch. Rather than wielding our weapon, we wield the TV remote, the game controller and our mobile phone. What have we got to show for our life? Spiritually distracted, discouraged and ineffective, we're almost dead on our feet. We are in desperate danger of falling asleep at the wheel.

Far be it from me to pretend to be a prophet, but even I, as blind as I am, can see a winter season almost upon us. There is torrential rain on the horizon and the roar of fire and water is on the wind. Perhaps this book is the final call. The final slap in the face. Our last chance.

> These are the words of the Amen, the faithful and true witness, the ruler of God's creation. I know your deeds, that you are neither cold nor hot. I wish you were either one or the other! So, because you are lukewarm—neither hot nor cold—I am about to spit you out of my mouth. You say, 'I am rich; I have acquired wealth and do not need a thing.' But you do not realize that you are wretched, pitiful, poor, blind and naked. I counsel you to buy from me gold refined in the fire, so you can become rich; and white clothes to wear, so you can cover your shameful nakedness; and salve to put on your eyes, so you can see.

> — REVELATION 3:14-18 NIV

You are worth more than you know. Your destiny is more than has ever entered your mind. Here in this book are the words of God, a salve so that perhaps at this last hour, you can finally start to see the world around you.

You must wake yourself up and get in the fight. Or, as fodder for the fire, you will not stand at all.

I'm sorry to be so abrupt and abrasive at the start. It is a rude way to start - and we've hardly even got to know each other! But the stakes are high, and I am convinced of what I have to show you. Every minute counts.

So, if you're still with me, let's begin.

From here on in, I want you to consider both the natural and the supernatural, but from the supernatural perspective. I expect that exploring things from the supernatural perspective will help you think about yourself from an objective viewpoint. It will help you consider the spiritual implications of your own actions and choices from an indirect and less directly confronting position. It will help you read the scriptures and understand your story within them.

Every occurrence in this world unfolds according to laws, laws that operate for the most part at a level where they're neither seen or understood by the people they govern.

In the supernatural world, these laws are seen and understood. These laws are somewhat like gravity, invisible yet unbreakable, predictable in that they always work, yet mysterious because we can't see the mechanics behind them.

So what are these laws? What is the supernatural world? And how does it all work together?

I'm glad you asked, because this is where we begin.

PART II
ORIENTATION

WHAT IS THE SUPERNATURAL
PLANE OF EXISTENCE?

T he supernatural plane of existence fits over the natural like a glove to a hand. It's all around everybody, all of the time, and it's invisible only for our inability to see. We'll call it SUPOX (SUpernatural Plane Of eXistence) for short.

The SUPOX is to a large extent, off the edge of the map for modern science because the interactions between the two planes appear to be neither predictable or repeatable. They in fact are, but at least half the factors determining their predictability are hidden to those who are blind, which most humans are, most of the time.

Scientists trying to quantify the SUPOX are fighting with one hand tied behind their back, largely because there is nobody in the SUPOX with a vested interest in the scientific community understanding that plane of existence.

> … what can be seen was made out of what cannot be seen …

— HEBREWS 11:3 CEV

> While we look not at the things which are seen, but at the things which are not seen; for the things which are seen are temporal, but the things which are not seen are eternal.
>
> Things that are seen don't last forever, but things that are not seen are eternal. That's why we keep our minds on the things that cannot be seen.

— 2 CORINTHIANS 4:18 NIV AND CEV, RESPECTIVELY

> Jesus told him, "I came to judge the people of this world. I am here to give sight to the blind and to make blind everyone who can see."
>
> When the Pharisees heard Jesus say this, they asked, "Are we blind?"
>
> Jesus answered, "If you were blind, you would not be guilty. But now that you claim to see, you will keep on being guilty."

— JOHN 9:39-41 CEV

> Can you fathom the mysteries of God?
> Can you probe the limits of the Almighty?
> They are higher than the heavens above—what can you do?
> They are deeper than the depths below—what can you know?
> Their measure is longer than the earth and wider than the sea.

— JOB 11:7-9 NIV

The SUPOX is larger than the natural plane of existence (which for simplicity we'll call the NAPOX, NAtural Plane Of eXistence), in that the NAPOX doesn't currently extend up into either heaven, the capital of God's kingdom, or down to the city of hell, the kingdom of the dead.

Collectively Mankind is the boss of earth, a realm positioned in the middle, and of this area, Mankind has control and dominion. And not just to the NAPOX but also to any area of the SUPOX connected to the NAPOX.

> Then God said, "Let us make mankind in our image, in our likeness, so that they may rule over the fish in the sea and the birds in the sky, over the livestock and all the wild animals, and over all the creatures that move along the ground."
>
> So God created mankind in his own image,
> in the image of God he created them;
> male and female he created them.
>
> God blessed them and said to them, "Be fruitful and increase in number; fill the earth and subdue it. Rule over the fish in the sea and the birds in the sky and over every living creature that moves on the ground."
>
> — GENESIS 1:26-28 NIV

> Submit yourselves, then, to God. Resist the devil, and he will flee from you.
>
> — JAMES 4:7 NIV

We will spend more time on the issue of authority later. For the moment, a sufficient summary is simply that God set

Mankind as having dominion over the earth and all connected to it.

> For our struggle is not against flesh and blood, but against the rulers, against the authorities, against the powers of this dark world and against the spiritual forces of evil in the heavenly realms.
>
> — EPHESIANS 6:12 NIV

Because the majority of Mankind is blind to the SUPOX connected to the NAPOX, it has become lawless, an area now occupied by the devil and his demons.

> "You will crawl on your belly
>   and you will eat dust
>   all the days of your life."
>
> — GENESIS 3:14 NIV

> How you have fallen from heaven, morning star, son of the dawn! You have been cast down to the earth, you who once laid low the nations!
>
> — ISAIAH 14:12 NIV

ANGELS, DEMONS AND THE HOLY SPIRIT

> Moreover, demons came out of many people, shouting, "You are the Son of God!" But he rebuked them and would not allow them to speak, because they knew he was the Messiah.
>
> — LUKE 4:41 NIV

So there are angels and demons? But of course.

Angels and demons are the primary actors in the SUPOX, or at least they were up until Jesus Christ joined mortal man's ranks. Since then, the Holy Spirit is alive and very active with anybody who puts their confidence in Jesus Christ. But more on that later.

Angels and demons are, in essence, the same, but now look to be very different creatures as a result of their decisions. An angel is something of a transmitter, radiating and channeling the power of God. In the absence of God's power, they don't die but rather stagnate, rot from the inside out. Demons are then like dead angels, animated but with no hope.

> In speaking of the angels he says, "He makes his angels spirits, and his servants flames of fire."
>
> — HEBREWS 1:7 NIV

> "Then He will also say to those on the left hand, 'Depart from Me, you cursed, into the everlasting fire prepared for the devil and his angels.'"
>
> — MATTHEW 25:41 NKJV

> God did not spare angels when they sinned, but sent them to hell, putting them in chains of darkness to be held for judgment.
>
> — 2 PETER 2:4 NIV

Angels are servants, and act on assignments given by God. Should God assign them to a human, and should that human pray or speak God's word, they also can act to support a human-given directive. Once again, this is an intentionally simple explanation; there is much more to say on this later.

> "Do you think I cannot call on my Father, and he will at once put at my disposal more than twelve legions of angels?"
>
> — MATTHEW 26:53 NIV

Are not all angels ministering spirits sent to serve those who will inherit salvation?

— HEBREWS 1:14 NIV

In those days I, Daniel, was mourning three whole weeks. I ate no pleasant bread. No meat or wine came into my mouth. I didn't anoint myself at all, until three whole weeks were fulfilled.

In the twenty-fourth day of the first month, as I was by the side of the great river, which is Hiddekel, I lifted up my eyes, and looked, and behold, there was a man clothed in linen, whose thighs were adorned with pure gold of Uphaz. His body also was like beryl, and his face as the appearance of lightning, and his eyes as flaming torches. His arms and his feet were like burnished bronze. The voice of his words was like the voice of a multitude.

I, Daniel, alone saw the vision; for the men who were with me didn't see the vision; but a great quaking fell on them, and they fled to hide themselves. So I was left alone, and saw this great vision. No strength remained in me; for my face grew deathly pale, and I retained no strength. Yet I heard the voice of his words. When I heard the voice of his words, then I fell into a deep sleep on my face, with my face toward the ground.

...

> Then he said to me, "Don't be afraid, Daniel; for from the first day that you set your heart to understand, and to humble yourself before your God, your words were heard. I have come for your words' sake."
>
> — DANIEL 10:2-9 & 12 WEB

Demons are servants turned insurgents, having joined the devil in the desperately flawed plan to overthrow God from the throne.

Now convicted of their failed coup attempt and forced out of heaven, they are making their last stand in the SUPOX that surrounds the NAPOX, an area that's supposed to be ruled by Mankind. Generally, they survive by feeding on human souls, a substitute for the life of God flowing directly through them.

> The word of the Lord came to me: "Son of man, prophesy against the shepherds of Israel; prophesy and say to them: 'This is what the Sovereign Lord says: Woe to you shepherds of Israel who only take care of yourselves!
>
> ...
>
> You have ruled them harshly and brutally. So they were scattered because there was no shepherd, and when they were scattered they became food for all the wild animals.
>
> — EZEKIEL 34:1-2 & 4-5 NIV

> Then war broke out in heaven. Michael and his angels fought against the dragon, and the dragon and his angels fought back. But he was

not strong enough, and they lost their place in heaven. The great dragon was hurled down— that ancient serpent called the devil, or Satan, who leads the whole world astray. He was hurled to the earth, and his angels with him.

— REVELATION 12:7-9 NIV

How you have fallen from heaven, morning star, son of the dawn! You have been cast down to the earth, you who once laid low the nations!

You said in your heart, "I will ascend to the heavens; I will raise my throne above the stars of God; I will sit enthroned on the mount of assembly, on the utmost heights of Mount Zaphon.

I will ascend above the tops of the clouds; I will make myself like the Most High."

But you are brought down to the realm of the dead, to the depths of the pit.

— ISAIAH 14:12-15 NIV

When under threat by angels or the Holy Spirit himself, demons hide behind complicit human hostages. To humans, should they be aware of them at all, they present as angels, perhaps even God himself.

Satan himself masquerades as an Angel of light.

— 2 CORINTHIANS 11:14 NIV

> The Spirit clearly says that in later times some will abandon the faith and follow deceiving spirits and things taught by demons.
>
> — 1 TIMOTHY 4:1 NIV

> "I [*Jesus Christ*] know about the slander of those who say they are Jews and are not, but are a synagogue of Satan."
>
> — REVELATION 2:9 NIV

> …[*the Jews*] protested. "The only Father we have is God himself."
>
> Jesus said to them, "If God were your Father, you would love me, for I have come here from God. I have not come on my own; God sent me. Why is my language not clear to you? Because you are unable to hear what I say. You belong to your father, the devil, and you want to carry out your father's desires."
>
> — JOHN 8:41-42 NIV

Angels' and demons' scope of activity is entirely governed by the Law of God. Like the law of gravity, there is no way to break such laws. An angel respects the intent of the law and operates within it for the glory of God. A demon twists the word of God into deception, and in doing so, inadvertently severs himself from his own life-source, the light and life of God.

In essence, the key thing to observe is that both angels and demons operate within the law. They are no more capable of defying the law than someone on earth might defy gravity.

> For I [*Paul*] am convinced that neither death nor life, neither angels nor demons, neither the present nor the future, nor any powers, neither height nor depth, nor anything else in all creation, will be able to separate us from the love of God that is in Christ Jesus our Lord.
>
> — ROMANS 8:38-39 NIV

The devil and his demons find their power entirely in the lie. They have no creative power; they have no ability to form things on their own. They can only take something God has already created, or something he has already said, and twist it. Through this means, humans can be tricked, and in their deception unintentionally offer up their soul as food.

> Be alert and of sober mind. Your enemy the devil prowls around like a roaring lion looking for someone to devour.
>
> — 1 PETER 5:8 NIV

Harvesting the remnant of God's breath from living humans is the means by which the devil and his fallen angels survive. For this reason, from the dawn of mankind to today's technological age, there is a continual push for sacrifice. From pagan rituals to the clinical reaping of fetal babies, these ideas are fanned into flame by hungry demonic powers. Sacrifice is the basis of a plentiful food supply.

"He [*the Devil*] was a murderer from the beginning, not holding to the truth, for there is no truth in him. When he lies, he speaks his native language, for he is a liar and the father of lies."

— JOHN 8:44 NIV

"The thief comes only to steal and kill and destroy"

— JOHN 10:10 NIV

The god of this age has blinded the minds of unbelievers, so that they cannot see the light of the gospel that displays the glory of Christ, who is the image of God.

— 2 CORINTHIANS 4:4 NIV

When you hide your face,
    they are terrified;
    when you take away their breath,
    they die and return to the dust.

When you send your Spirit,
    they are created,
    and you renew the face of the ground.

— PSALM 104:29 NIV

As long as I have life within me,
    the breath of God in my nostrils,
    my lips will not say anything wicked,
    and my tongue will not utter lies.

— JOB 27:2-4 NIV

Ultimately death is a result of separation from God, and this will be discussed in more depth later. The key point to note now is that death has been weaponized – fallen angels have the ability to separate humans from God with a lie. Death is similar to poison in that, for the most part, it won't kill somebody immediately but decomposes a person over time. Prior to Christ, mankind was the walking dead.

> So I find this law at work: Although I want to do good, evil is right there with me. For in my inner being I delight in God's law; but I see another law at work in me, waging war against the law of my mind and making me a prisoner of the law of sin at work within me. What a wretched man I am!

— ROMANS 7:21-24 NIV

> The mind governed by the flesh is death.

— ROMANS 8:6 NIV

> If you live according to the flesh, you will die.

— ROMANS 8:13 NIV

HOW DO ANGELS AND DEMONS INTERACT WITH PHYSICAL OBJECTS?

A ngels and demons have no dominion over the NAPOX, except in the instance it's given to them by God or mankind. As a result, outside of being on assignment by God, angels and demons are only able to interact with physical objects with mankind's express consent. For this reason the devil and his demons outwork their schemes 'through' people.

> The prince of the power of the air, the spirit who now works in the sons of disobedience.
>
> — EPHESIANS 2:2 NKJV

If angels or demons are given consent and they see fit to do so, the power they can exert in the NAPOX is superior to that of our human experience. They are not bound by the laws of the natural world.

> Some Jews who went around driving out evil spirits tried to invoke the name of the Lord

Jesus over those who were demon-possessed. They would say, "In the name of the Jesus whom Paul preaches, I command you to come out." Seven sons of Sceva, a Jewish chief priest, were doing this. One day the evil spirit answered them, "Jesus I know, and Paul I know about, but who are you?" Then the man who had the evil spirit jumped on them and overpowered them all. He gave them such a beating that they ran out of the house naked and bleeding.

— ACTS 19:13-16 NIV

For demons to affect an outcome in the NAPOX, the physical action is conducted through the human host.

Angels are never permitted to indwell a human. If they did, they would be taking a place reserved for the Holy Spirit, a place reserved for God himself.

WHO IS THE HOLY SPIRIT?

The Holy Spirit is God, and God is the Holy Spirit. The Holy Spirit is he who envelops and reignites a spiritually dead person to bring them back to life.

"I [John] baptize you with water, but he [Jesus] will baptize you with the Holy Spirit."

— MARK 1:8 NIV

I will remove from you your heart of stone and give you a heart of flesh. And I will put my Spirit in you and move you to follow my decrees and be careful to keep my laws.

— EZEKIEL 36:26-27 NIV

Even on my servants, both men and women, I will pour out my Spirit in those days.

— JOEL 2:29 NIV

The Holy Spirit is both powerful without limit, and gentle without judgment, at the same time. He only comes to a human with their invitation. He will not manipulate or cajole a person into opening the door. If invited in, he's only fully intertwined with them for the time which they wish him to be so.

> "Here I am! I [*Jesus Christ*] stand at the door and knock. If anyone hears my voice and opens the door, I will come in and eat with that person, and they with me."
>
> — REVELATION 3:20 NIV

> All day long I have held out my hands
>   to an obstinate people,
>   who walk in ways not good,
>   pursuing their own imaginations—
>   a people who continually provoke me
>   to my very face …
>
> — ISAIAH 65:2-3 NIV

When the Holy Spirit is intertwined with a human's spirit, they are capable of exercising complete authority in both the SUPOX and the NAPOX. When in perfect synchronization, they are an unstoppable combination.

> "To the one who is victorious and does my will to the end, I [*Jesus Christ*] will give authority over the nations— that one 'will rule them with an iron scepter and will dash them to pieces like pottery'—just as I have received authority from my Father."

— REVELATION 2:26-27 NIV

> You, however, are not in the realm of the flesh but are in the realm of the Spirit, if indeed the Spirit of God lives in you.

— ROMANS 8:9 NIV

> "I have given you authority to trample on snakes and scorpions and to overcome all the power of the enemy; nothing will harm you."

— LUKE 10:19 NIV

SYNCHRONIZATION COMPARED
TO POSSESSION

W hen the Holy Spirit intertwines with a human
spirit, a phenomenon best understood
as *synchronization*, it is like a hand to a glove.
Mankind was designed for this from the very beginning.

> The body, however, is not meant for sexual
> immorality but for the Lord, and the Lord for
> the body.

— 1 CORINTHIANS 6:13 NIV

If there is any flaw in the design, it's simply this – in the
absence of the Holy Spirit synchronization can be exploited
by fallen angels. When this happens it is called *demon
possession*.

Demon possession is simply that – a demon, or in many
cases several of them, occupying the human in the location
designed for the Holy Spirit.

"When an impure spirit comes out of a person, it goes through arid places seeking rest and does not find it. Then it says, 'I will return to the house I left.' When it arrives, it finds the house unoccupied, swept clean and put in order. Then it goes and takes with it seven other spirits more wicked than itself, and they go in and live there. And the final condition of that person is worse than the first. That is how it will be with this wicked generation."

— MATTHEW 12:43-45 NIV

HOW DO ANGELS AND DEMONS
INTERACT WITH PEOPLE?

ngels and demons make themselves scarce in the
NAPOX for entirely different reasons.

Angels are well aware that every human being
is precious to God and must, at all costs, be given a chance to
be reconciled to him. How an angel might relate to a human
is governed by this overarching objective, and highlights two
substantial risks.

The first is simply this - any human who meets an angel
is awed to such an extent they almost universally fall head-
first into angel-worship. Their attention, their focus and
their adoration swing sharply away from God whom they
cannot see to the angel whom they have just seen. The bible
is full of examples, even among the apostles themselves.

> I, John, am the one who heard and saw all these
> things. And when I heard and saw them, I fell
> down to worship at the feet of the angel who
> showed them to me.

— REVELATION 22:8 NLT

> Do not let anyone who delights in false humility and the worship of angels disqualify you. Such a person also goes into great detail about what they have seen; they are puffed up with idle notions by their unspiritual mind.
>
> — COLOSSIANS 2:18 NIV

The second risk is similar but the opposite. If a human incorrectly comes to the conclusion that the work of God is the work of the devil, that human becomes dangerously irretrievable.

> ...the teachers of religious law who had arrived from Jerusalem said, "He [*Jesus*] is possessed by Satan, the prince of demons. That's where he gets the power to cast out demons."
>
> Jesus called them over and responded with an illustration. "How can Satan cast out Satan?" he asked.
>
> ...
>
> "I tell you the truth, all sin and blasphemy can be forgiven, but anyone who blasphemes the Holy Spirit will never be forgiven. This is a sin with eternal consequences."
>
> — MARK 3:20–23 & 28–29 NLT

Should a human perceive divine activity and come to the wrong conclusion, it will lead to harm not good, especially in the presence of demons keenly watching for an opportunity to twist a human's perception of the truth. Accordingly, angels avoid interacting with humans in ways that would cause a person to become directly aware of them, even though their interactions are frequent. This is not a difficult task, as humans, being mostly blind, are quick to put divine interactions down to coincidence, luck, and good fortune.

> Do not forget to show hospitality to strangers, for by so doing some people have shown hospitality to angels without knowing it.
>
> — HEBREWS 13:2 NIV

> "See that you do not despise one of these little ones. For I tell you that their angels in heaven always see the face of my Father in heaven."
>
> — MATTHEW 18:10 NIV

Demons avoid making humans aware of them for an entirely different reason. Demons are hiding out in a territory not their own. Without Mankind giving them permission to dwell in the SUPOX enveloping the NAPOX, they would have to leave.

In Genesis 1:28 God gave this area over to Mankind's authority. *"Rule over the fish in the sea and the birds in the sky and over every living creature that moves on the ground."* And when God cursed the devil he put him under this same area of Man's authority. The devil was cursed as an animal, a creature under Mankind's rule, and he was confined there in the dust for the remainder of his days.

> ...the Lord God said to the snake:
> "Because of what you have done,
> you will be the only animal
> to suffer this curse—
> For as long as you live,

> you will crawl on your stomach
> and eat dirt.
> You and this woman
> will hate each other;
> your descendants and hers
> will always be enemies.
> One of hers will strike you
> on the head,
> and you will strike him
> on the heel."

> — GENESIS 3:14-15 CEV

If the devil is to be credited with anything it is this: he is no quitter. For thousands of years, flying in the face of this curse, he never tired of dominating Mankind. For those watching, it looked like he was invulnerable. Until Christ.

God declared that it would be Eve's offspring that would crush his head. Indeed, by and through Christ reconnecting Mankind to God, that is now again possible.

> "I have given you authority to trample on snakes and scorpions and to overcome all the power of the enemy; nothing will harm you."

> — LUKE 10:19 NIV

In the 20th century, the devil's strategy changed to one of *evading detection*. They set about convincing humans not only that God did not exist, but that they too were only a figment of primitive man's imagination. And as a strategy, it was pure genius. Once convinced *demons* were not there, people set about *demonizing each other* for the evils on earth. Evil of course, that was the devil's doing. Neighbor turned on neighbor, city on city, country on country. On the whole, this strategy delivered the devil a bumper harvest, an almost endless supply of unguarded souls for food.

> They shall be wasted with hunger,
>> Devoured by pestilence and bitter destruction;
>> I will also send against them the teeth of beasts,
>> With the poison of serpents of the dust.
>> The sword shall destroy outside;
>> There shall be terror within
>
> — DEUTERONOMY 32:24-25 NKJV

The devil's horde is a pestilence to Mankind. They are beasts that devour, and I am continually confronted by the many ways they can feed. In the global west, in my mind's eye I see them feeding like worms in an orchid; there is a delay between the point in which the parasite enters the victim and the resulting rot becomes visible. A docile and compliant human is an easy meal, putting up little resistance as the fallen burrows in, consuming them from the inside out. Like the putrefaction caused by larvae within delicate fruit, it won't stay undetected for long. Pus yellows beneath the skin, healthy hues give way to a dappled patchwork of disease, and eventually the filth within bursts the thin and mortal membrane that holds it back.

> His strength is starved,
>> And destruction is ready at his side.
>> It devours patches of his skin;
>> The firstborn of death devours his limbs.
>> He is uprooted from the shelter of his tent,

And they parade him before the king of terrors.

— JOB 18:12-14 NKJV

Cultivating a huge crop of suitable candidates has been one of the devil's crowning achievements. He might have achieved an equilibrium if it wasn't for a consuming hatred of God that perpetually drives him to war, a war he cannot win.

The dragon stood in front of the woman who was about to give birth, so that it might devour her child the moment he was born. She gave birth to a son, a male child, who "will rule all the nations with an iron scepter." And her child was snatched up to God and to his throne.

— REVELATION 12:4-5 NIV

WHAT IS A PERSON?

❧

> The Lord ... forms the human spirit within a person.

— ZECHARIAH 12:1 NIV

A human is a spirit and soul bound within a body so perfectly they are inseparable. A human's body allows them to operate in the NAPOX, whereas their spirit allows them to operate (see, act, feel) in the SUPOX. For most humans, their spirit is either dead or desperately underdeveloped, like an emaciated infant. As it happens, maturity of a person's spirit doesn't come automatically with age, but with intentional feeding and nourishment.

> "You say, 'I am rich. I have everything I want. I don't need a thing!' And you don't realize that you are wretched and miserable and poor and blind and naked."

— REVELATION 3:17 NLT

> We have much to say about this, but it is hard to make it clear to you because you no longer try to understand. In fact, though by this time you ought to be teachers, you need someone to teach you the elementary truths of God's word all over again. You need milk, not solid food! Anyone who lives on milk, being still an infant, is not acquainted with the teaching about right-eousness. But solid food is for the mature, who by constant use have trained themselves to distinguish good from evil.

— HEBREWS 5:11-14 NIV

A human's spirit dies almost at the moment of birth. Like a flame without oxygen, when exposed to the suffocating sin-saturated NAPOX, it flickers and is extinguished, reduced to nothing more than smoldering potential.

> The light of the righteous shines brightly,
>   but the lamp of the wicked is snuffed out.

— PROVERBS 13:9 NIV

> But Jesus told him, "Follow me now. Let the
> spiritually dead bury their own dead."

— MATTHEW 8:22 NLT

A human spirit is 'reborn' when reignited by the Spirit of God.

> "Flesh gives birth to flesh, but the Spirit gives
> birth to spirit."

— JOHN 3:6 NIV

A human's soul is the breath of God, the life of God within a human. It is who they are, independent of the body and independent of the spirit.

> For the word of God is alive and active. Sharper
> than any double-edged sword, it penetrates even
> to dividing soul and spirit, joints and marrow; it
> judges the thoughts and attitudes of the heart.

— HEBREWS 4:12 NIV

> "Do not be afraid of those who kill the body but
> cannot kill the soul. Rather, be afraid of the One
> who can destroy both soul and body in hell."

— MATTHEW 10:28 NIV

For orientation, this basic summary will suffice. We will unpack all aspects of the human being in-depth, in the section titled 'The Human' towards the middle of this book.

HOW DO ANGELS AND DEMONS INTERACT WITH THE HOLY SPIRIT?

❧

Angels take their instructions, their assignments, from God and from Jesus Christ.

> Are not all angels ministering spirits sent to serve those who will inherit salvation?

— HEBREWS 1:14 NIV

> "Do you think I cannot call on my Father and he will at once put at my disposal more than twelve legions of angels?"

— MATTHEW 26:53 NIV

When confronted, demons either flee or hide behind human hostages. When using a human shield they will assert their right to be there by the person's invitation or instruction. The demon is well aware that the human needs only to breathe the name of Jesus and that 'permission' will be considered null and void. Demons in the presence of the Holy Spirit are not dissimilar to a hunted animal in the presence of a hunter. They might hide perfectly still or suddenly burst into hysterics with fierce displays of thrashing aggression. They are no more capable of saving themselves than a bird that flaps in the face of a lion.

> The impure spirit shook the man violently and came out of him with a shriek.
>
> — MARK 1:26 NIV

> When he saw Jesus from afar, he ran and bowed down to him, and crying out with a loud voice, he said, "What have I to do with you, Jesus, you Son of the Most High God? I adjure you by God, don't torment me." For he said to him, "Come out of the man, you unclean spirit!"
>
> He asked him, "What is your name?"
>
> He said to him, "My name is Legion, for we are many." He begged him much that he would not send them away out of the country. Now on the mountainside there was a great herd of pigs feeding. All the demons begged him, saying, "Send us into the pigs, that we may enter into them."
>
> At once Jesus gave them permission. The unclean spirits came out and entered into the pigs. The herd of about two thousand rushed down the steep bank into the sea, and they were drowned in the sea.
>
> — MARK 5:6-13 WEB

AUTHORITY

⁂

As established earlier, Mankind has been given authority over the NAPOX and corresponding SUPOX. The complicating factor is this: authority is held *collectively,* not individually. The result, then, from the moment Mankind fell, is a perpetual struggle for control, power and supremacy.

Whether a husband and wife struggle for control of their relationship or two nations fight over money, resources and power, it's the same dynamic playing out.

> Then God said, "Let us make Mankind in our image, in our likeness, so that they may rule over the fish in the sea and the birds in the sky, over the livestock and all the wild animals, and over all the creatures that move along the ground."
>
> — GENESIS 1:26 NIV

Once again, take a moment to note that when the devil,

the serpent, moved into the area of the SUPOX connected to earth, he moved into an area where Mankind had been given God-given control.

> God blessed them and said to them, "Be fruitful and increase in number; fill the earth and subdue it. Rule over the fish in the sea and the birds in the sky and over every living creature that moves on the ground."

— GENESIS 1:28 NIV

Authority is easily transferred, and the devil understands this better than most. Authority can be traded away, especially if a suitably enticing bounty is offered. Legitimate trade, then, was the means by which the devil acquired mankind's authority, so he and his legions might exercise control on their behalf.

> You were anointed as a guardian cherub,
>   for so I ordained you.
>
>   …
>   Through your widespread trade
>   you were filled with violence,
>   and you sinned.

— EZEKIEL 28:14 & 16 NIV

Perhaps it seems absurd that mankind would sell their authority. In my opinion - that would be a reasonable assessment. It was absurd. It still is absurd. But when you understand this transaction suddenly much of the world makes sense; the mess that humanity has become is built on this trade.

> ...there was no one like Ahab who sold himself to do wickedness in the sight of the Lord...

— 1 KINGS 21:25 NKJV

> For your iniquities you have sold yourselves,
>   And for your transgressions your mother has been put away.

— ISAIAH 50:1 NKJV

> For thus says the Lord:
>   "You have sold yourselves for nothing,
>   And you shall be redeemed without money."

— ISAIAH 52:3 NKJV

PRAYER AND THE EXERCISE OF AUTHORITY

❦

For the most part humans have infant spirits, and so, because of this, prayer is the primary mechanism by which they can effect a change in their area of the SUPOX. Prayer to God, especially when in alignment with the word of God, is heard by God and brings angels into assignment.

> Cornelius stared at him in fear. "What is it, Lord?" he asked. The Angel answered, "Your prayers and gifts to the poor have come up as a memorial offering before God."
>
> — ACTS 10:4 NIV

> ...the Angel said to him: "Do not be afraid, Zechariah; your prayer has been heard. Your wife Elizabeth will bear you a son, and you are to call him John."
>
> — LUKE 1:13 NIV

A human with a mature spirit and fully intertwined with the Holy Spirit, does not need prayer or the help of angels to effect a change in the SUPOX. They simply issue the command, and it will come into effect.

> Peter, fastening his eyes on him, with John, said, "Look at us." He listened to them, expecting to receive something from them. But Peter said, "I have no silver or gold, but what I have, that I give you. In the name of Jesus Christ of Nazareth, get up and walk!" He took him by the right hand and raised him up. Immediately his feet and his ankle bones received strength. Leaping up, he stood and began to walk. He entered with them into the temple, walking, leaping, and praising God.
>
> — ACTS 3:4-8 WEB

> "I tell you the truth, if you had faith even as small as a mustard seed, you could say to this mountain, 'Move from here to there,' and it would move. Nothing would be impossible."
>
> — MATTHEW 17:32 NLT

Exercising authority in the SUPOX as it relates to an individual only depends on that individual. In so far as they have not assigned their authority to somebody else, they are able to exert control over their own area of the SUPOX. Exerting control of the SUPOX as it relates to a group of people, however, is an entirely different matter.

At the group level it requires consensus. Dominion and authority, as we have discussed, was given to Mankind collectively. Exercising authority in the SUPOX as it relates to a family, a town, or even a nation depends on the degree to which its people are in unity. Unity unshackles God-given authority in all its fullness, either for good or evil.

> Husbands, in the same way be considerate as you live with your wives, and treat them with respect as the weaker partner and as heirs with you of the gracious gift of life, so that nothing will hinder your prayers.
>
> — 1 PETER 3:7 NIV

God gave Mankind this authority, a gift inseparable from that of free will, and he will not contradict it. The *collective* will for good or evil is the ultimate factor determining what unfolds in the SUPOX.

> And because of their unbelief, he [*Jesus*] couldn't do any miracles among them except to place his hands on a few sick people and heal them.
>
> — MARK 6:5 NLT

This being said, it only takes unity among a small group of people who are fully intertwined with the Holy Spirit to exert extraordinary and disproportionate power in the SUPOX. The presence of the Holy Spirit is a force multiplier, one that should never be underestimated.

> Each one of you will put to flight a thousand of the enemy, for the Lord your God fights for you, just as he has promised.

— JOSHUA 23:10

> "Again, truly I tell you that if two of you on earth agree about anything they ask for, it will be done for them by my Father in heaven."

— MATTHEW 18:19 NIV

> Dear brothers and sisters, I urge you in the name of our Lord Jesus Christ to join in my struggle by praying to God for me.

— ROMANS 15:30 NLT

> How good and pleasant it is
>   when God's people live together in unity!
>   …
>   For there the Lord bestows his blessing,
>   even life forevermore.

— PSALM 133:1&3 NIV

LAWS

All your words are true; all your righteous laws
are eternal.

— PSALM 119:160 NIV

od's laws are not confined to either the SUPOX or
the NAPOX, but rather they transcend all planes
of existence. They have full effect in both but
materialize differently in each. I imagine that the most
obvious difference is that, while they are mostly invisible in
the NAPOX, they are visible in the SUPOX.

Operating in something like a vast ecosystem, there are as
many laws as there are types of plants on earth. Those who
devote themselves to finding and living by these laws are in
pursuit of what we call *wisdom*.

"Yahweh [*God*] possessed me [*wisdom*] in the
beginning of his work,
    before his deeds of old.

I was set up from everlasting, from the
beginning,
before the earth existed.
When there were no depths, I was born,
when there were no springs abounding with
water.
Before the mountains were settled in place,
before the hills, I was born ..."

— PROVERBS 8:22-25 WEB

Wisdom is the application of life choices according to God's law. Abiding by God's law is often called wisdom.

The first way to understand God's laws is to contrast them with the laws drawn up by human lawmakers and enforced in a nation's court of law.

For the most part, human societal laws are drafted at the inauguration of a nation. From that point, from time to time, new laws are added and old ones modified. In contrast, God's laws are fixed, woven into the fabric of what was created from the very start. They are eternal and unchanging.

"I tell you the truth, until heaven and earth
disappear, not even the smallest detail of God's
law will disappear until its purpose is achieved."

— MATTHEW 5:18 NLT

Human societal laws generally come into effect when somebody breaks them. They are, for the most part, punitive. Human laws have very little value for somebody who is abiding by them.

God's laws are almost entirely the opposite, being laws

that by their very nature bring life, health, wholeness, healing, wealth and protection to those who abide in them.

> The law of the Lord is perfect,
>> refreshing the soul.

— PSALM 19:7 NIV

> Wisdom will multiply your days
>> and add years to your life.
> If you become wise, you will be the one to benefit.
> If you scorn wisdom, you will be the one to suffer.

— PROVERBS 9:11-12 NLT

The laws of God are like capillaries through which the life of God flows into that which he created. In and of themselves laws are lifeless, but what they enable is connection to life itself. They are conduits connecting people to God's power, God's goodness and God's life.

> "You search the Scriptures because you think they give you eternal life. But the Scriptures point to me [*Jesus Christ*]! Yet you refuse to come to me to receive this life."

— JOHN 5:39-40 NLT

The act of breaking God's laws is simply to sever the connection. The lawbreaker breaks their connection to the sustenance that flows from God to all living things.

> Doesn't wisdom cry out?
>> Doesn't understanding raise her voice?
>> …
>> "Now therefore, my sons, listen to me,
>> for blessed are those who keep my ways.
>> Hear instruction, and be wise.
>> Don't refuse it.
>> Blessed is the man who hears me,
>> watching daily at my gates,
>> waiting at my door posts.
>> For whoever finds me, finds life,
>> and will obtain favor from Yahweh.
>> But he who sins against me wrongs his own
> soul.
>> All those who hate me love death."

— PROVERBS 8:1 & 32-36 WEB

> It shall happen, if you shall listen diligently to Yahweh your God's voice, to observe to do all his commandments which I command you today, that Yahweh your God will set you high above all the nations of the earth. All these blessings will come upon you, and overtake you, if you listen to Yahweh your God's voice.
>> You shall be blessed in the city, and you shall be blessed in the field.
>> You shall be blessed in the fruit of your body, the fruit of your ground, the fruit of your animals, the increase of your livestock, and the young of your flock.
>> Your basket and your kneading trough shall be blessed.

You shall be blessed when you come in, and you shall be blessed when you go out.

Yahweh will cause your enemies who rise up against you to be struck before you. They will come out against you one way, and will flee before you seven ways.

Yahweh will command the blessing on you in your barns, and in all that you put your hand to. He will bless you in the land which Yahweh your God gives you.

....

But it shall come to pass, if you will not listen to Yahweh your God's voice, to observe to do all his commandments and his statutes which I command you today, that all these curses will come on you and overtake you.

You will be cursed in the city, and you will be cursed in the field.

Your basket and your kneading trough will be cursed.

The fruit of your body, the fruit of your ground, the increase of your livestock, and the young of your flock will be cursed.

You will be cursed when you come in, and you will be cursed when you go out.

Yahweh will send on you cursing, confusion, and rebuke in all that you put your hand to do, until you are destroyed and until you perish quickly, because of the evil of your doings, by which you have forsaken me.

— DEUTERONOMY 28:1-8 & 15-20 WEB

The second way to understand God's laws is to contrast them with the laws of the natural world.

An example would be Newton's law of universal gravitation. What Newton described was a phenomenon, the force of gravity, a law that had been in effect since the beginning.

Laws like this are unbreakable. The best humans can hope to do is to improve their understanding of the law. And this happened when Einstein penned his General Theory of Relativity, a work which superseded that of Newton. But the law of gravity was never broken, it was simply better understood.

In the same way our understanding of God's laws can be revised and improved, but the law itself can never be broken. It is a fool's errand to believe God's laws become obsolete over time.

> "Scripture cannot be broken."
>
> — JOHN 10:35 NKJV

In the context of the eternal and unchangeable nature of God's laws, then, it is interesting to consider peoples' preoccupation with 'breaking' them. To think that you've succeeded in living outside God's law is like holding your breath underwater - the inaccuracy of your belief will be evident enough in time.

> "You have said terrible things about me," says the Lord.
>
> "But you say, 'What do you mean? What have we said against you?'
>
> "You have said, 'What's the use of serving God? What have we gained by obeying his commands ...?

...

Then those who feared the Lord spoke with each other, and the Lord listened to what they said. In his presence, a scroll of remembrance was written to record the names of those who feared him and always thought about the honor of his name.

"They will be my people," says the Lord of Heaven's Armies. "On the day when I act in judgment, they will be my own special treasure. I will spare them as a father spares an obedient child. Then you will again see the difference between the righteous and the wicked, between those who serve God and those who do not."

— MALACHI 3:13-18 NLT

Laws of the natural world, once understood, can be harnessed either for good or evil. $E=mc^2$ for example, Einstein's theory of mass-energy equivalence, paved the way for everything from smoke detectors and hospital diagnostics to nuclear weapons.

In a similar fashion, an understanding of God's laws can be put to use by residents of the NAPOX and SUPOX for both good and evil purposes.

I found that the very commandment that was intended to bring life actually brought death. For sin, seizing the opportunity afforded by the commandment, deceived me, and through the commandment put me to death.

— ROMANS 7:10-11 NIV

> Words of wisdom are like the stick a farmer uses to make animals move. These sayings come from God, our only shepherd, and they are like nails that fasten things together.
>
> — ECCLESIASTES 12:11 CEV

The devil, fooling the masses into living outside God's laws, is devastatingly effective at rendering people fodder for his demonic legions.

> Descendants of Jacob, I am the Lord All-Powerful, and I never change. That's why you haven't been wiped out, even though you have ignored and disobeyed my laws ever since the time of your ancestors. But if you return to me, I will return to you.
>
> And yet you ask, "How can we return?"
>
> You people are robbing me, your God. And, here you are, asking, "How are we robbing you?"
>
> You are robbing me of the offerings and of the ten percent that belongs to me. That's why your whole nation is under a curse. I am the Lord All-Powerful, and I challenge you to put me to the test. Bring the entire ten percent into the storehouse, so there will be food in my house. Then I will open the windows of heaven and flood you with blessing after blessing. I will also stop locusts from destroying your crops and keeping your vineyards from producing. Everyone of every nation will talk about how I

have blessed you and about your wonderful land. I, the Lord All-Powerful, have spoken!

— MALACHI 3:6-12 CEV

Unlike the laws of the natural world, which exist outside any moral code, God's laws are all oriented for the good of Mankind.

The evidence of this is simple. In any given year, there are plenty of situations where gravity caused the death of both good and bad people, with no bias either way. In contrast, God's laws bring only life to those who abide by them.

> Happy is the man who finds wisdom,
> the man who gets understanding.
> For her good profit is better than getting silver,
> and her return is better than fine gold.
> She is more precious than rubies.
>
> None of the things you can desire are to be compared to her.
> Length of days is in her right hand.
> In her left hand are riches and honor.
> Her ways are ways of pleasantness.
> All her paths are peace.
> She is a tree of life to those who lay hold of her.
> Happy is everyone who retains her.
>
> By wisdom Yahweh founded the earth.
> By understanding, he established the heavens.

By his knowledge, the depths were
broken up,
and the skies drop down the dew.

My son, let them not depart from your eyes.
Keep sound wisdom and discretion:
so they will be life to your soul,
and grace for your neck.
Then you shall walk in your way securely.
Your foot won't stumble.

— PROVERBS 3:13-23 WEB

Death only finds a foothold when God's law is rejected,
twisted, distorted, and broken.

How can you say, "We are wise,
for we have the law of the Lord,"
when actually the lying pen of the scribes
has handled it falsely?
The wise will be put to shame;
they will be dismayed and trapped.

— JEREMIAH 8:8-9 NIV

For whoever finds me [*wisdom*], finds life,
and will obtain favor from Yahweh [*God*].
But he who sins against me wrongs his own
soul.
All those who hate me love death."

— PROVERBS 8:35-36 WEB

SIN, AND THE
MISUNDERSTANDING THEREOF

❧

S in, and the way it is understood in modern society, is a foreign concept in the SUPOX.

In the ecosystem of a forest, concepts like 'transgression,' 'offense,' 'sin', and 'debt' have no meaning. The forest operates, instead, on the basis of life and death.

It is the same in the SUPOX.

Sin, or breaking the law, is like a diver who breaks the pipe that connects his mouthpiece to the oxygen tank. The action, how he broke the pipe, whether it was an accident or intentional, and the mitigating circumstances: these are in and of themselves not important. What is important is the consequence: that his connection to his source of life has been cut. He will die when he runs out of oxygen.

Even though 'breaking the pipe' is what we would call sin, it's the fact he ran out of oxygen that killed the diver.

It is being deprived of the Spirit of God that killed Mankind.

For our diver, the focus is on how to repair the pipe. If you have ever tried to fix a broken chair, a broken cup, or broken water bottle, you will be aware of the unfortunate truth: fixing is always harder, if at all even possible.

> What then? Are we better than they? No, in no way. For we previously warned both Jews and Greeks that they are all under sin. As it is written,
>> "There is no one righteous;
>> no, not one.
>> There is no one who understands.
>> There is no one who seeks after God.
>> They have all turned away.
>> They have together become unprofitable.
>> There is no one who does good,
>> no, not so much as one."
>> "Their throat is an open tomb.
>> With their tongues they have used deceit."
>> "The poison of vipers is under their lips."
>> "Their mouth is full of cursing and bitterness."
>> "Their feet are swift to shed blood.
>> Destruction and misery are in their ways.
>> The way of peace, they haven't known."
>> "There is no fear of God before their eyes."
> Now we know that whatever things the law says, it speaks to those who are under the law, that every mouth may be closed, and all the world may be brought under the judgment of God. Because by the works of the law, no flesh will be justified in his sight; for through the law comes the knowledge of sin.

> — ROMANS 3:9-20 WEB

When Moses received the Levitical Law and delivered it to the Israelites in the desert, in one sense it was instructions for repairing the pipe. It described perfect 'alignment.' It presented a blueprint by which Mankind could be connected with God's life. From that point on, however, an unexpected and devastating reality became clear. No one is capable of following those instructions by their own hand. Nobody has the capacity to repair their connection to God and reconnect to the life he provides.

> Surely I was sinful at birth,
> sinful from the time my mother conceived me.

— PSALM 51:5 NIV

> But those who depend on the law to make them right with God are under his curse, for the Scriptures say, "Cursed is everyone who does not observe and obey all the commands that are written in God's Book of the Law." So it is clear that no one can be made right with God by trying to keep the law.

— GALATIANS 3:10-11 NLT

The arrival of Jesus Christ among Mankind changed the dynamic substantially. Prior to Jesus, any small sin, any break in the pipe at all, severed the connection. It didn't matter how much a person got right, because they were measured by what they got *wrong.* A small break is still a break.

> You can't pick and choose in these things, specializing in keeping one or two things in

God's law and ignoring others. The same God who said, "Don't commit adultery," also said, "Don't murder." If you don't commit adultery but go ahead and murder, do you think your non-adultery will cancel out your murder? No, you're a murderer, period.

— JAMES 2:8-11 MSG

So, offering a bypass to the old pipe, Jesus Christ completely upended the system. He didn't offer a fix, he offered a replacement: His life, through the Holy Spirit, within us *permanently*.

"But those who drink the water I [*Jesus Christ*] give will never be thirsty again. It becomes a fresh, bubbling spring within them, giving them eternal life."

— JOHN 4:14 NLT

So then, Jesus Christ offers a way *to be not dead*, and to reject him is to reject life. Because of this, since Jesus Christ, there is only one sin that matters: to reject him. And it makes sense. To breathe again, to be reconnected to the oxygen tank, nothing else matters.

It is the difference between life and death.

"When he [*the Holy Spirit*] comes, he'll expose the error of the godless world's view of sin ... He'll show them that their refusal to believe in me [*Jesus Christ*] is their basic sin."

— JOHN 16:8-9 MSG

Jesus Christ made a way for a person to return to their intended created form ... Spiritkind.

In simple terms, and as things currently stand, everybody on earth starts off already dead. They are the spirit-dead. Their mortal bodies are powered by the remnant of God's initial 'bringing the dust to life' breath within them.

> Then the Lord God formed the man from the dust of the ground. He breathed the breath of life into the man's nostrils, and the man became a living person.
>
> — GENESIS 2:7 NLT

The life of God is so powerful that this single breath endures for decades. It powers the flesh to renew and regenerate, like a machine with a perpetual-motion engine within it. Mankind, then, is alive with God's initial breath in their mortal bodies, but unable to breathe and slowly suffocating. Their spirit is dead and their mortal days are numbered.

> ... the Lord said, "I won't let my life-giving breath remain in anyone forever. No one will live for more than one hundred twenty years."
>
> — GENESIS 6:3 CEV

> ... the body without the spirit is dead...
>
> — JAMES 1:26 NIV

How then can we understand our situation?

Imagine the diver, disconnected from the oxygen and now thrashing about in a panic, desperately trying to stem the flow of water into his mask. Before he realizes it, he has broken the pipe in three more places and cracked his breather. The situation is dire. Each of these actions is a sin that further separates him from the oxygen he needs to live.

In the NAPOX this truth is mostly obscured, where wealth and success can hide reality. No such deception is possible in the SUPOX. But here is the point. For the onlooking angels, the focus is not on how many mistakes he made. The focus is on if he will embrace the solution in time.

> I [*Jesus Christ*] am the Gate. Anyone who goes through me will be cared for—will freely go in and out, and find pasture. A thief is only there to steal and kill and destroy. I came so they can have real and eternal life, more and better life than they ever dreamed of.
>
> — JOHN 10:9-10 MSG

Embracing God's life through Jesus Christ nullifies the effect of sin in the past, and the Holy Spirit transforms the spirit-dead to Spiritkind. But none of this is to say that 'sin' no longer has any effect.

The fact is, perhaps surprisingly, sin's capacity to kill becomes *more* obvious after a person becomes Spiritkind. The spirit-dead can't get any more dead. One break or one hundred breaks, it makes very little functional difference in terms of the spirit. But once the spirit is rekindled, it takes only small things to mute the flame. The fact that sin deprives the newly alive spirit of oxygen becomes apparent. Within Spiritkind, sin's ability to *kill the spirit* becomes obvious.

> Listen! The Lord's arm is not too weak to save you,
>> nor is his ear too deaf to hear you call.
>> It's your sins that have cut you off from God.

— ISAIAH 59:1-2 NLT

Sin always separates from the life of God. But irrespective of the size and scale of the break, Spiritkind have the Holy Spirit who administers grace and forgiveness, repairing the damage immediately upon the person's request. They have no need to suffer through suffocation.

> The Spirit and the bride say, "Come." Let anyone who hears this say, "Come." Let anyone who is thirsty come. Let anyone who desires drink freely from the water of life.

— REVELATION 22:17 NLT

But the rule is simple. Sin always breaks a person's connection to life. But the gift of God through Jesus Christ is reconnection.

> If we claim to be without sin, we deceive ourselves and the truth is not in us. If we confess our sins, he is faithful and just and will forgive us our sins and purify us from all unright-eousness.

— 1 JOHN 1:8-10 NIV

> Remain in me, and I will remain in you. For a branch cannot produce fruit if it is severed from

the vine, and you cannot be fruitful unless you remain in me.

"Yes, I am the vine; you are the branches. Those who remain in me, and I in them, will produce much fruit. For apart from me you can do nothing. Anyone who does not remain in me is thrown away like a useless branch and withers. Such branches are gathered into a pile to be burned.

— JOHN 15:4-6 NLT

To sin is to die. To continue to sin and refuse to repent is to choose death.

But thanks to Jesus Christ and the Holy Spirit there is another path.

PART III
LIFE AND DEATH

VERSAL VERSUS VERSION

❧

> "Why is my [*Jesus Christ*] language not clear to you? Because you are unable to hear what I say. You belong to your father, the devil, and you want to carry out your father's desires. He was a murderer from the beginning, not holding to the truth, for there is no truth in him. When he lies, he speaks his native language, for he is a liar and the father of lies. Yet because I tell the truth, you do not believe me!"

— JOHN 8:43-45 NIV

What is set out in this chapter is a summary of Versal and Version, fundamental concepts for those who want to understand the SUPOX, its inhabitants and how they interact. They are so important that there is an entire annexure dedicated to their understanding at the end of the book.

Now, as with other concepts in this book, Versal and

Version are my own terms. They are not found in the Bible. As far as I'm aware, there are no words for what I'm attempting to describe in this chapter. In giving them each a unique English handle, I hope to unshackle their truth from the cliches that would otherwise inevitably end up tangled in their understanding.

In the NAPOX, there are thousands of languages. In the SUPOX, there are only two.

The original and the first is Versal. Versal is Truth. I present it to you as a language only for the fact that in the NAPOX a better term doesn't exist. Versal supersedes every attribute of every language. It is no less than the substance of everything seen in the NAPOX. It's complete, universal, and like glass with no imperfections. It is completely invisible. It is not defined by words, grammar or sentence structure, and it is unencumbered by the faculties of the mind so prevalent in the NAPOX.

Versal is pure, without blemish, and true.

> Day unto day utters speech,
> And night unto night reveals knowledge.
> There is no speech nor language
> Where their voice is not heard.
> Their line has gone out through all the earth,
> And their words to the end of the world.
>
> — PSALM 19:2-4 NKJV

The second language is Version, the language of lies. Version is an invention of the devil. He was its first speaker and the innovator behind its many functions. As the 'Father of Lies,' he is the head of all who rebel against God.

At its essence Version is untruth. It is the perversion of Versal, and as such has similar attributes. It is opaque. It is not defined by words, grammar or sentence structure. Rather, it is like a lens that distorts and separates the components of light. Version makes things seem different from that which they really are.

The devil's power, in fact his only source of power, is that which he derives from Version.

In the NAPOX, everybody speaks a combination of Versal and Version. For those who find themselves at home with Version, the majority of Mankind, to hear and understand Versal becomes an impossibility.

> But the people's minds were hardened, and to this day whenever the old covenant is being read, the same veil covers their minds so they cannot understand the truth.
>
> ...
>
> But whenever someone turns to the Lord, the veil is taken away. For the Lord is the Spirit, and wherever the Spirit of the Lord is, there is freedom.
>
> — 2 CORINTHIANS 3:14 & 16-17 NLT

For the handful of humans who persistently seek the truth, the door will be opened. In time they will not just see, hear, and speak Versal, but through it they will discover freedom.

> "Keep on seeking, and you will find. Keep on knocking, and the door will be opened to you. For everyone who asks, receives. Everyone who seeks, finds. And to everyone who knocks, the door will be opened."

— MATTHEW 7:7-8 NLT

See the annexure 'language of lies' to explore Versal and Version in full.

LIFE BY THE BREATH OF GOD

⚜

G od himself is life. He is the one and only life force in both the SUPOX and the NAPOX. Death is not anything except the absence of God. Like dark-ness to light, death is simply the absence of life.

> Then the Lord said, "My Spirit will not contend with humans forever, for they are mortal; their days will be a hundred and twenty years."

> — GENESIS 6:3 NIV

All things in the NAPOX were designed to be powered by God's life indwelling within, and none more so than the human body. God's life breathed into Mankind is so powerful it endures for hundreds and thousands of years, a perpetual power-source for the renewal and regeneration of the human race.

Since the fall of Mankind things have begun to come apart at the seams. In the millennia since Mankind severed the connection with God, all created things have slowly and steadily begun to grind back down into the dust.

> For all creation is waiting eagerly for that future day when God will reveal who his children really are. Against its will, all creation was subjected to God's curse. But with eager hope, the creation looks forward to the day when it will join God's children in glorious freedom from death and decay. For we know that all creation has been groaning as in the pains of childbirth right up to the present time. And we believers also groan, even though we have the Holy Spirit within us as a foretaste of future glory, for we long for our bodies to be released from sin and suffering. We, too, wait with eager hope for the day when God will give us our full rights as his adopted children, including the new bodies he has promised us.

— ROMANS 8:19-23 NLT

THE GATE FROM DEATH TO LIFE

Born in the dust of the NAPOX, Jesus Christ created a pathway from death to life. God's own son was born into Mankind's mortality, and he became the gate through which one can pass from mortality to immortality.

Injecting himself into the lethal wound, into death itself, he permanently and irreversibly cured it.

> And now he has made all of this plain to us by the appearing of Christ Jesus, our Savior. He broke the power of death and illuminated the way to life and immortality through the Good News.
>
> — 2 TIMOTHY 1:10 NLT

> "Yes, I am the gate. Those who come in through me will be saved. They will come and go freely and will find good pastures."

— JOHN 10:9 NLT

To access this cure, to pass through this gate, humans must themselves now make a choice.

> "You can enter God's Kingdom only through the narrow gate. The highway to hell is broad, and its gate is wide for the many who choose that way. But the gateway to life is very narrow and the road is difficult, and only a few ever find it."

— MATTHEW 7:13-14 NLT

DOMINION AND FREE WILL

⁂

One of the oldest of God's laws in effect is that of dominion, choice, and free will.

In the beginning Mankind was, by decree, set over all of the NAPOX and the SUPOX surrounding it. Mankind was given dominion over the earth.

> God blessed them and said to them, "Be fruitful and increase in number; fill the earth and subdue it."
>
> — GENESIS 1:28 NIV

Within this dominion came a second gift: free will. The irrevocable freedom to choose, forever and in perpetuity. Mankind was given the right to collective and individual self-determination.

> ...the Lord God commanded the man, "You are free..."

— GENESIS 2:16 NIV

Woven into the fabric of creation was everything Mankind required. Mankind had the power, the freedom and the authority to bring into effect a kingdom in any shape they chose.

But enter the devil, and Mankind fell.

SPIRITKIND

U sing Version, the devil conquered Mankind. Once tricked into separating from God, the devil used their gifts of dominion and freedom as weapons against them. And it was devastating. In a single blow the Devil took down Mankind in their entirety. One and all they became the spirit-dead.

Until Christ.

Christ, injected into dead humanity, effectively split Mankind into two. From within the ranks of the spirit-dead he brought forward a new, alive-for-the-first-time, Spiritkind.

Opening a pathway from mortality to immortality, a pathway from death to life, Christ made it such that all humans need to do *is choose*. That ancient decree, that first and most powerful gift of *choice* then became all that is required for a person to cross from the spirit-dead to Spiritkind.

> "Most assuredly, I say to you, he who hears My word and believes in Him who sent Me has

everlasting life, and shall not come into judgment, but has passed from death into life."

— JOHN 5:24 NKJV

"For God so loved the world that he gave his one and only Son, that whoever believes in him shall not perish but have eternal life."

— JOHN 3:16 NIV

Jesus Christ, who he is and what he did, sits at the junction of history. He is the pivot point for good and evil, his hour is the hour at which the tide of history turns.

The message of Christ, his descent to dust and then triumphant ascent to heaven, is the difference between life and death for every human. It should then be no surprise that his story is the conclusion to which this book is headed. His chapter is the culmination of this book. It is the most important chapter for every reader.

What lies between here and there is context. A context critical to understanding the size and scale of what is at stake.

THE SPIRIT-DEAD

In the NAPOX the spirit-dead and Spiritkind walk side by side and for the most part look identical. They can be told apart by their actions, but discernment in the short term is anything but scientific.

> "A tree is identified by its fruit. If a tree is good, its fruit will be good. If a tree is bad, its fruit will be bad."
>
> — MATTHEW 12:33 NLT

In the SUPOX, however, I imagine there is a clear distinction. The spirit-dead are dull and grey, something with the form of that once alive but now hardened, lifeless and decaying. Spiritkind in contrast are luminescent, bathed in the flame of the Spirit and glow ever brighter as they mature.

> So all of us who have had that veil removed can see and reflect the glory of the Lord. And the Lord—who is the Spirit—makes us more and

more like him as we are changed into his glorious image.

— 2 CORINTHIANS 3:18 NLT

The visible difference between the two factions of Mankind, however, is only the start. The inconvenient truth is that comfortable coexistence between the spirit-dead and Spiritkind is simply not possible.

Spiritkind has a future whereas the spirit-dead do not. Spiritkind are designated by God to become the dominant force, heirs of his own kingdom and rulers of the earthen realm. The spirit-dead are condemned not just by their failure to transform into Spiritkind but by providing safe lodging for evil. Within their own hearts they not only shelter all sorts of corruption, but they have also given over the earth's SUPOX as a refuge for the devil and his fallen angels.

They have assigned themselves, and the earth beneath their feet, as fuel for the flames.

Mankind is aware of this separation only in so far as they can *smell* it. The devil and his fallen followers are not so blind, and they both see and understand the difference. To the spirit-dead the scent of life is repugnant, it stirs up the stagnant stench of their own perishing flesh. Recoiling as the odor fills their lungs, the fallen have no trouble whipping up an irrational but visceral hatred of Spiritkind. Carrying the aroma of heaven, Spiritkind finds themselves persecuted - viciously maligned for no reason other than that they are alive.

> But thanks be to God, who always leads us as captives in Christ's triumphal procession and uses us to spread the aroma of the knowledge of

him everywhere. For we are to God the pleasing aroma of Christ among those who are being saved and those who are perishing. To the one we are an aroma that brings death; to the other, an aroma that brings life.

— 2 CORINTHIANS 2:14-16 NIV

"If the world hates you, keep in mind that it hated me first. If you belonged to the world, it would love you as its own. As it is, you do not belong to the world, but I have chosen you out of the world. That is why the world hates you. Remember what I told you: 'A servant is not greater than his master.' If they persecuted me, they will persecute you also. If they obeyed my teaching, they will obey yours also. They will treat you this way because of my name, for they do not know the one who sent me."

— JOHN 15:18-21 NIV

PART IV
THE HUMAN

THE NATURE AND MECHANICS
OF A HUMAN

❧

> Then the Lord God formed a man from the dust
> of the ground and breathed into his nostrils the
> breath of life, and the man became a living
> being.

— GENESIS 2:7 NIV

A human is a spirit and soul bound to a body, so intricately interwoven to be inseparable. The human body allows the person to operate in the NAPOX, with their spirit allowing them to operate (see, feel and act) in the SUPOX. For most humans, however, the spirit part of them is either dead or like an infant just born, blind, malnourished, and underdeveloped. Maturity of a person's spirit does not come with age but with intentional feeding and nourishment.

> The Lord, who stretches out the heavens, who lays the foundation of the earth, and who forms the human spirit within a person.

— ZECHARIAH 12:1 NIV

> Brothers and sisters, I could not address you as people who live by the Spirit but as people who are still worldly—mere infants in Christ. I gave you milk, not solid food, for you were not yet ready for it. Indeed, you are still not ready. You are still worldly. For since there is jealousy and quarreling among you, are you not worldly? Are you not acting like mere humans? For when one says, "I follow Paul," and another, "I follow Apollos," are you not mere human beings?

— 1 CORINTHIANS 3:1-4 NIV

> You say, 'I am rich. I have everything I want. I don't need a thing!' And you don't realize that you are wretched and miserable and poor and blind and naked.

— REVELATION 3:17 NLT

The spirit within a human dies almost at the moment of birth. Like the tiny flame of a candle covered by a blanket, it never stands a chance. Smothered in a sin-saturated NAPOX and deprived of oxygen, it vanishes as quickly as it came. The person joins the ranks of the *spirit-dead*, surviving on what breath is left from that given at the beginning. When every cell in their body is exhausted, their fragile grip on mortal life will be at an end.

> ... the widow who lives only for pleasure is spiritually dead even while she lives.

— 1 TIMOTHY 5:6 NIV

> ... Jesus told him, "Follow me now. Let the spiritually dead bury their own dead."

— MATTHEW 8:22 NLT

A human spirit is 'reborn' when the smoldering remnant of their spirit is touched by the Spirit of God. At this point the human, spiritually born anew, crosses over from being among the spirit-dead to being Spiritkind.

> "Flesh gives birth to flesh,
> but the Spirit gives birth to spirit."

— JOHN 3:6 NIV

> ... he [*Jesus Christ*] is the beginning and the first-born from among the dead, so that in everything he might have the supremacy.

— COLOSSIANS 1:18 NIV

A human soul, or *nephesh* to use a Hebrew term, is the manifestation of God's breath within a person. Like the life within a plant, it is not something you can find by dissecting the body. The evidence of its existence is in the fact it is *alive.* A person's *nephesh* is who they are, their personality, their sense of humor, it is their sense of personhood, independent of the body and independent of the spirit.

> For the word of God is alive and active. Sharper than any double-edged sword, it penetrates even to dividing soul and spirit, joints and marrow; it judges the thoughts and attitudes of the heart.

— HEBREWS 4:12 NIV

A human heart is a fleshy organ that has both a function in the NAPOX and a function in the SUPOX. In addition to its central role of powering the body, the heart provides a human with willpower and intentionality. It delivers the body energy and the soul motivation, the necessary elements for a person to seek life.

> Keep your heart with all diligence,
> For out of it spring the issues of life.

— PROVERBS 4:23 NKJV

THE SOUL AND SPIRIT

⨋

odern society has only a childlike idea of what a soul or spirit might be, mostly because neither are things that can be poked or prodded with a scalpel. For many, spirit and soul are interchangeable terms and simply mean the unique, intangible, and non-physical aspects of a person. But they are not the same.

A person's soul, their *nephesh,* is nothing like their spirit.

I imagine that at the conception of a child, the *nephesh* is almost nothing at all. Nothing but the essence of life itself; God's breath and a set of unique instructions carried within it. It is something like DNA for who the person will become. It is a gift, the raw *potential for life* in its most perfect and uncorrupted form.

When developed, the *nephesh* of a human is intricate, complex, and if properly formed, exquisitely beautiful. Like a snowflake of sentient life, it is an ecosystem shaped by a person's history, intentions, actions, beliefs, and current potential for good or evil, imbued with the breath of God. It is the very essence of who a person is. It is a perfect mirror in the SUPOX for the person's life in the NAPOX. Layered, each part is interwoven in such a way that many things can be hidden within the fabric of its fold.

> If there is a natural body, there is also a spiritual body.
>
> — 1 CORINTHIANS 15:44 NIV

For the more literal minded among you these ideas might be a bridge too far. However, if you've enough of an open mind to stay with me for a moment, we can hold this theory I'm putting forward up to the light of scripture and test its worth. Somebody had to imagine that the Americas existed to set sail and ultimately find them. And perhaps, in a similar way, you'll find merit in these ideas as you read on.

I imagine in the SUPOX a person's *nephesh* would fill out the frame of their torso. Spreading out from the axis drawn between their head and heart, it fills out their physical form continuing even to the point of forming a garment. For some, these are beautiful, extending like a living and organic flower, up from the heart and around the head like a crown. In some instances these would resemble a tiara or a woven piece of armor. And yet for others, especially the spirit-dead, it is a wild bramble, complete unkempt chaos through which they can't even see.

> They are vines without grapes;
> fig trees without figs or leaves.
>
> — JEREMIAH 8:13 CEV

There are aspects of a *nephesh* that fit inside the body's form, and these would be commonly understood as a person's *soul*. There are also aspects of a *nephesh* that extend beyond the frame of the body, forming something like a garment, and this is a person's *character*. These are features that make up and distinguish an individual, features that can generally be perceived by other humans.

> "She [*the Church*] has been given the finest of pure white linen to wear."
> For the fine linen represents the good deeds of God's holy people.
>
> — REVELATION 19:8 NLT

> "Now listen to the explanation of the parable about the farmer planting seeds: The seed that fell on the footpath represents those who hear the message about the Kingdom and don't understand it. Then the evil one comes and snatches away the seed that was planted in their hearts. The seed on the rocky soil represents those who hear the message and immediately receive it with joy. But since they don't have deep roots, they don't last long. They fall away as soon as they have problems or are persecuted for believing God's word. The seed that fell among the thorns represents those who hear God's word, but all too quickly the message is crowded out by the worries of this life and the lure of wealth, so no fruit is produced. The seed that fell on good soil represents those who truly hear and understand God's word and produce a harvest of thirty, sixty, or even a hundred times as much as had been planted!"
>
> — MATTHEW 13:18-23 NLT

The *nephesh* of a person grows and changes in perfect synchronization with the person as they progress through life. In so far as it is true that a person is the sum total of their decisions, the same can be said for their *nephesh*. Seeds planted in their heart grow and give form to the *nephesh*, both inside and outside the outline of their physical form.

The *nephesh* was intended to be covered by the luminescent flame of the Spirit, and a person's naked soul never meant to be seen. Sensing exposure, a person will try to cover themselves with anything, lies and deception being in easy reach. Covering nakedness in this way produces a wiry and thorn-laden thicket, something that over time will harden into the permanent exterior.

> So remove your dark deeds like dirty clothes, and put on the shining armor of right living.
>   … clothe yourself with the presence of the Lord Jesus Christ.
>
> — ROMANS 13:12 & 14 NLT

> Jeshua's clothing was filthy as he stood there before the angel. So the angel said to the others standing there, "Take off his filthy clothes." And turning to Jeshua he said, "See, I have taken away your sins, and now I am giving you these fine new clothes."
>
> — ZECHARIAH 3:3-6 NLT

For a human who is Spiritkind, the spirit can be clearly seen in the SUPOX surrounding the *nephesh* like flame. In my mind's eye, it is like fire that burns from the heart both upward and downward, covering the *nephesh* from top to bottom. The Spirit makes many parts of the *nephesh* luminescent, pure and radiant. Angels watching the first spark of the Spirit's flame count themselves extraordinarily fortunate – they are witnessing the birth of a brand new Spiritkind. An extraordinary transformation. That which was dead, now blazing with life.

> "In the same way, I tell you, there is rejoicing in the presence of the angels of God over one sinner who repents."
>
> — LUKE 15:10 NIV

I will likely never see this while I am bound in my body on earth, but I imagine there to be nothing in the NAPOX that compares to this moment. The dead spirit within a child, nothing but smoldering embers. And then, from seemingly nowhere, the wind of the Spirit arrives, breathed from above like pure oxygen. The person is baptized into flame, the gentle caress of the Spirit surrounding the soul, and for the first time since birth, *ignition!* The person's own newly born spirit springs to life, fanned into flame and leaping in pure joy. Burning together with the Holy Spirit the flames twist into one, inexorably linked and *alive*.

> I [*John the Baptist*] baptize you with water for repentance. But after me comes one who is more powerful than I, whose sandals I am not worthy to carry.

> He [*Jesus Christ*] will baptize you with the Holy Spirit and fire. His winnowing fork is in his hand, and he will clear his threshing floor, gathering his wheat into the barn and burning up the chaff with unquenchable fire."

> — MATTHEW 3:11-12 NIV

Baptism by the Holy Spirit is a fiery immersion that turns the dead and decaying layers of a person's *nephesh* to ash. It is a purging, a complete removal of all that is abhorrent and filthy. When a person repents, the fire that the Holy Spirit brings is that of cleansing.

> This means that anyone who belongs to Christ has become a new person. The old life is gone; a new life has begun!

> — 2 CORINTHIANS 5:17 NLT

> The Lord will wash the filth from beautiful Zion … with the hot breath of fiery judgment.

> — ISAIAH 4:4 NLT

> …if we are living in the light, as God is in the light, … the blood of Jesus, his Son, cleanses us from all sin.
>
> …if we confess our sins to him, he is faithful and just to forgive us our sins and to cleanse us from all wickedness.

> — 1 JOHN 1:7 & 9 NLT

A human with a beautiful *nephesh* is a valuable find, partly because they have channeled the buffeting of violent and merciless circumstances to refine their quality and value, a remarkable and rare outcome. Among Spiritkind, these are well prepared for life in the SUPOX when their mortal body fails.

> Therefore we do not lose heart. Though outwardly we are wasting away, yet inwardly we are being renewed day by day. For our light and momentary troubles are achieving for us an eternal glory that far outweighs them all. So we fix our eyes not on what is seen, but on what is unseen, since what is seen is temporary, but what is unseen is eternal.
>
> — 2 CORINTHIANS 4:16-18 NIV

> Don't be concerned about the outward beauty of fancy hairstyles, expensive jewelry, or beautiful clothes. You should clothe yourselves instead with the beauty that comes from within, the unfading beauty of a gentle and quiet spirit, which is so precious to God.
>
> — 1 PETER 3:3-4 NLT

In the absence of the Holy Spirit, there is no enveloping protection. What was a healthy *nephesh* can become tinder-dry, like flakes of paper. Within the delicate but dead layers can hide all sorts of sickness and disease. Love of money is like hidden corrosion. Worry is like a vine that constricts and strangles. Lust, like a damp and pungent rot. Anger like hot coals that smolder and burn.

> Their lives became full of every kind of wicked-
> ness, sin, greed, hate, envy, murder, quarreling,
> deception, malicious behavior, and gossip.
>
> — ROMANS 1:29 NLT

God's intention, however, is through his Holy Spirit to make of each person's *nephesh* a remarkable, unique and heavenly garment. Most famously, laced within the intricate folds of each are the 'fruits of the spirit', pure and living gems. Love, joy, peace, patience, kindness, goodness and faithfulness; in the SUPOX they shine with clear color and beauty, unique to every person through whom they are produced.

> So I say, let the Holy Spirit guide your lives.
> Then you won't be doing what your sinful
> nature craves.
>   ...
> the Holy Spirit produces this kind of fruit in
> our lives: love, joy, peace, patience, kindness,
> goodness, faithfulness,
>
> — GALATIANS 5:16 & 22 NLT

It strikes me that love, possibly the most delicate, the most fragrant and the most valuable part of a person's *nephesh*, is also the fabric upon which all else holds in place. It is the vine upon which all other fruit hangs.

> Therefore, as God's chosen people, holy and
> dearly loved, clothe yourselves with compassion,
> kindness, humility, gentleness and patience.
>   ...

And over all these virtues put on love, which binds them all together in perfect unity.

— COLOSSIANS 3:12&14 NIV

… this is my prayer: that your love will flourish and that you will not only love much but well.

— PHILIPPIANS 1:9 MSG

When a person dies, their *nephesh* does not disappear with the passing of their mortal body. Rather, like something that passes through the flames of the refiner's fire, all that is impure is burnt away, and only that which is pure survives. What remains on the other side of death, be it everything or nothing at all, is what the person will have as a garment for the next age.

For we know that if the earthly tent we live in is destroyed, we have a building from God, an eternal house in heaven, not built by human hands. Meanwhile we groan, longing to be clothed instead with our heavenly dwelling, because when we are clothed, we will not be found naked. For while we are in this tent, we groan and are burdened, because we do not wish to be unclothed but to be clothed instead with our heavenly dwelling, so that what is mortal may be swallowed up by life.

Now the one who has fashioned us for this very purpose is God, who has given us the Spirit as a deposit, guaranteeing what is to come.

— 2 CORINTHIANS 5:1-5 NIV

TESTING BY FIRE

As introduced in the previous chapter, the baptism of the Holy Spirit purifies the person's *nephesh* with fire. This fire, however, is not the only type of fire that will touch the human soul.

Ultimately, the substance of each and every person's life will be put to fire. The quality of each person will be judged by the flames.

> For with fire and with his sword
> the Lord will execute judgment on all people

— ISAIAH 66:16 NIV

"Everyone will be tested with fire."

— MARK 9:49 NLT

There are many different sources of fire, each with different characteristics.

The first type of fire, and in contrast with the fire of the Holy Spirit, is the fire that a person brings to bear on themselves. This fire will not bring new life. It will not bring cleansing or purification but is a forerunner for judgment. This is the fire of consequence, and the only good that may come from it is correction.

> Our tongues are small too, and yet they brag about big things. It takes only a spark to start a forest fire! The tongue is like a spark. It is an evil power that dirties the rest of the body and sets a person's entire life on fire with flames that come from hell itself.
>
> — JAMES 3:5-6 CEV

> For wickedness burns as the fire;
>   It shall devour the briers and thorns,
>   And kindle in the thickets of the forest;
>   They shall mount up like rising smoke.
>
> — ISAIAH 9:18 NKJV

> Therefore, as tongues of fire lick up straw and as dry grass sinks down in the flames, so their roots will decay and their flowers blow away like dust; for they have rejected the law of the Lord Almighty and spurned the word of the Holy One of Israel.
>
> — ISAIAH 5:24 NIV

The fire of consequence comes in many forms.

Envy and lust bring the fires of correction, but these burn

without flame. They are like rot that eats a person from the inside out.

> A heart at peace gives life to the body, but envy rots the bones.
>
> — PROVERBS 14:30 NIV

> And the men, instead of having normal sexual relations with women, burned with lust for each other. Men did shameful things with other men, and as a result of this sin, they suffered within themselves the penalty they deserved.
>
> — ROMANS 1:27 NLT

Anger creates a smoldering heat, and prolonged anger dries out the *nephesh*.

> For a fire is kindled in My anger,
>   And shall burn to the lowest hell …
>
> — DEUTERONOMY 32:22 NKJV

Anger paves the way for fire, but it is the words that a person speaks that provide the spark of ignition.

> It takes only a spark to start a forest fire! The tongue is like a spark. It is an evil power that dirties the rest of the body and sets a person's entire life on fire with flames that come from hell itself.
>
> — JAMES 3:5-6 CEV

> A scoundrel plots evil, and on their lips it is like a scorching fire.

— PROVERBS 16:27 NIV

A person can, in the NAPOX, look entirely together, respectable and upright. But in the SUPOX no such deception is possible. The smoke of the fire smoldering in their *nephesh* follows them wherever they go.

> "But I promise you that if you are angry with someone, you will have to stand trial. If you call someone a fool, you will be taken to court. And if you say that someone is worthless, you will be in danger of the fires of hell."

— MATTHEW 5:22 CEV

Ill-gotten wealth also acts something like acid, burning a person's *nephesh* but without flame. The final effect, tinder-dry ash, is the same as if it had been burnt by fire.

> Your money has rusted, and the rust will be evidence against you, as it burns your body like fire. Yet you keep on storing up wealth in these last days. You refused to pay the people who worked in your fields, and now their unpaid wages are shouting out against you. The Lord All-Powerful has surely heard the cries of the workers who harvested your crops.

— JAMES 5:3-4 CEV

The glowing crimson and soot-black fires of consequence

look nothing like that of the Holy Spirit, nor is the outcome the same. Though fire from the Holy Spirit is similar in that it consumes the impure, it stands alone in the life that it brings in the aftermath. The purging fire of the Holy Spirit is a required precursor and catalyst for new life. Only the Holy Spirit's flame brings cleansing, only the fire of God makes a person pure.

> He will sit like a refiner of silver, burning away the dross. He will purify the Levites, refining them like gold and silver, so that they may once again offer acceptable sacrifices to the Lord.
>
> — MALACHI 3:3 NLT

> I will bring that group through the fire
> and make them pure.
> I will refine them like silver
> and purify them like gold.
> They will call on my name,
> and I will answer them.
> I will say, 'These are my people,'
> and they will say, 'The Lord is our God.'"
>
> — ZECHARIAH 13:9 NLT

After the searing flames have passed there comes new life. Like a forest after fire, that in place of what was diseased and rotting brings forth healthy young trees and flowers, the human *nephesh,* once cleansed, can be born anew, growing in perfect purity within the Holy Spirit's envelope of protection.

I will give them an undivided heart and put a new spirit in them; I will remove from them their heart of stone and give them a heart of flesh. Then they will follow my decrees and be careful to keep my laws. They will be my people, and I will be their God.

— EZEKIEL 11:19-20 NIV

THE HUMAN HEART

The human heart, remarkable in its intricacy, design, and function, exists both in the NAPOX and the SUPOX simultaneously, much in the same way as the human itself. In the NAPOX, the heart is a muscle central to a human's survival, and as everybody knows, it is responsible for moving blood throughout the body. In the SUPOX, the heart is the origin of *willpower* and *intentionality;* it is the powerhouse behind motivation and desire. These NAPOX and SUPOX functions are inexorably linked; they energize a person for the pursuit of life in both physical and spiritual planes of existence.

Contrary to popular belief, the heart is not a moral compass or some sort of inbuilt guide which humans can follow to find ultimate health and happiness. Nothing could be further from the truth.

If anything, the heart can be understood as inherently and single-mindedly selfish. Its energies are expended solely in the pursuit of life for its host, the life of the human being to whom it belongs. With few exceptions, it pursues this goal to the exclusion of all others.

And so, for that reason, understanding the heart is of paramount importance.

HOW DOES THE HUMAN HEART WORK?

T he heart has a simple-by-design preoccupation with the survival of its host. As a physical organ, it has but one function: to pump blood for just one body, and not stop at any cost. In the SUPOX, the heart provides the willpower and intentionality required for its owner to seek life sustaining inputs. Not just food, oxygen, shelter, and companionship, but anything else the mind determines to be fundamental for survival. Furthermore, in the SUPOX, the heart also provides the willpower and intentionality to avoid things that threaten the person's survival. For example, the heart can instantly produce an almost superhuman amount of willpower to swim away from a shark, even if previously the person could barely tread water.

Although complex, a person's heart operates on a straightforward transactional basis. It registers positive emotions such as pleasure, excitement or companionship as good for the body, and registers negative emotions such as fear or pain as bad for the body. Each of these events is stored in the heart's muscle memory. Remembering each instance, the heart both craves for more of the good and seeks, by any means, to avoid the bad.

> "Wherever your treasure is, there the desires of your heart will also be."

> — MATTHEW 6:21 NLT

The heart is not rational, moral, or capable of making value judgments. In both the NAPOX and the SUPOX it is simply a muscle, inseparable from the human's mortal flesh. But that by no means makes it unimportant. It is equally the gateway for life and the gateway for corruption.

Once corrupted, humans tend to set their hearts on *treasure* instead of *life*. For example, a man might set his heart on getting a new car, a new pay raise, or a new girlfriend. A woman might set her heart on a new handbag, a new pair of shoes, or a new husband. The heart is put to use by the carnal mind and diligently gets to work, providing the willpower to obtain whatever the eyes have set upon, both rational and irrational.

DECEIVED BY THE HEART

⚜

> Truly the hearts of the sons of men are full of
> evil; madness is in their hearts while they live …

— ECCLESIASTES 9:3 NKJV

The heart both feeds and is fed by the body. It provides willpower and intention, and in return, is the recipient of being fed joy, happiness, pleasure. Tasting pleasure, the human heart then derives strength from acquiring more of this pleasure. This simple cycle can be seen in effect when a child discovers something tasty such as a peach. Upon tasting, the heart quickly provides the willpower to acquire *more*, and upon each acquisition, is temporarily satisfied. Precisely the same effect can be observed when the child discovers candy. In both instances, the heart provides the willpower to acquire *more*. It doesn't matter if the pleasure is good or bad; the heart makes no distinction. Sex, whether within marriage or with a prostitute, can feed the cycle in the same way, with the heart providing the intentionality to acquire more without moral prejudice.

This symbiotic relationship puts the heart in a unique position to take their host captive, especially those spirit-dead. The heart's place in the human construct makes it capable of deceiving its host, and for the most part, it does this without detection.

> ...when you are being tempted, do not say, "God is tempting me." God is never tempted to do wrong, and he never tempts anyone else. Temptation comes from our own desires, which entice us and drag us away. These desires give birth to sinful actions. And when sin is allowed to grow, it gives birth to death.
>
> — JAMES 1:13-15 NLT

CHANGE-OF-HEART

The heart is, of course, only a muscle, and therefore subject to the human who owns it. But as the power plant that provides the willpower and self-determination to change, the heart can easily hold its host hostage.

> The heart is deceitful above all things,
> And desperately wicked;
> Who can know it?

— JEREMIAH 17:9 NKJV

Any human attempting to affect a change-of-heart has a monumental challenge on their hands – it is an endeavor with terrible odds. Even when a person identifies their heart's desire as abjectly evil, they will almost always initially lack sufficient willpower to change it. The heart, with a corrupted sense of self-preservation, will always fail to provide the willpower required for such a change.

For this reason, the human heart provides the perfect hiding place for seeds of evil to take root.

> "What comes out of a person is what defiles them. For it is from within, out of a person's heart, that evil thoughts come—sexual immorality, theft, murder, adultery, greed, malice, deceit, lewdness, envy, slander, arrogance and folly. All these evils come from inside and defile a person."
>
> — MARK 7:20-21 NIV

HARNESSING THE HUMAN HEART

⁂

Discipline, especially for hearts that are still developing their bank of muscle-memories, is a key to humans achieving a degree of control. Remarkably, even spirit-dead humans can achieve control of their heart should training begin as a child.

> Whoever spares the rod hates their children,
>   but the one who loves their children is careful to discipline them.
>
> — PROVERBS 13:24 NIV

> Those who disregard discipline despise themselves, but the one who heeds correction gains understanding.
>
> — PROVERBS 15:32 NIV

A disciplined child will ultimately find their heart develops a healthy rhythm that forms a resistance to evil seeds taking root. Over time, an undisciplined child finds their heart unruly, substantially more powerful than they are, and with almost no resistance to evil seeds. These humans will be ruled by every foul and evil thing that finds lodging within them.

> Do not withhold correction from a child,
> For if you beat him with a rod,
> he will not die.
> You shall beat him with a rod,
> And deliver his soul from hell.

— PROVERBS 23:13-16 NKJV

The principle is then simple. The first step to health is for a human to continually train their heart. Everybody, even the spirit-dead, can make a habit of heart training, and develop within them a healthy functioning heart that delivers willpower and intentionality for *wellness*, regardless of the circumstances.

> Keep your heart with all diligence,
> For out of it spring the issues of life.

— PROVERBS 4:23 NKJV

TRANSFORMATION OF A
HUMAN HEART

Transformation of a human's heart is only possible through two external inputs: discipline, which we have covered already, and the Holy Spirit. Discipline becomes less effective as humans grow old. Even for a young heart, discipline cannot bring complete renewal, but for an old and hardened heart it is almost impossible.

The only option for transformation, then, is the Holy Spirit.

The Holy Spirit is the means by which a heart can be transformed, but he will only operate in so far as he is given permission. On one end of the spectrum, and even for humans who are only partially submitted, he will enable transformation by providing the willpower and intentionality that the corrupted heart fails to deliver. The Holy Spirit provides a person the power they require to transform their own unwilling heart. By this means, the Holy Spirit provides humans the opportunity to turn their heart toward God, something their heart is incapable of doing on its own.

> … the Holy Spirit helps us in our weakness.

— ROMANS 8:26 NLT

> So I say, let the Holy Spirit guide your lives. Then you won't be doing what your sinful nature craves. The sinful nature wants to do evil, which is just the opposite of what the Spirit wants. And the Spirit gives us desires that are the opposite of what the sinful nature desires. These two forces are constantly fighting each other, so you are not free to carry out your good intentions. But when you are directed by the Spirit, you are not under obligation to the law of Moses.
>
> …
>
> Since we are living by the Spirit, let us follow the Spirit's leading in every part of our lives.

— GALATIANS 5:16-18 & 25 NLT

On the other end of the spectrum, for a fully yielded person, the Holy Spirit will bring to bear something that resembles a full heart transplant. At the point that a new spirit is birthed within them, the flame destroys the old heart by fire. Amidst the ashes of the old, a brand new heart is kindled.

> I will give them one heart, and I will put a new spirit within them, and take the stony heart out of their flesh, and give them a heart of flesh, that they may walk in My statutes and keep My judgments and do them; and they shall be My people, and I will be their God.

— EZEKIEL 11:19-20 NKJV

THE MYTH OF LOVE

The human heart is not designed to produce such things as love, peace, joy and kindness. True 'fruits of the spirit' have their origin as their name suggests, in a reborn spirit.

> But the Holy Spirit produces this kind of fruit in our lives: love, joy, peace, patience, kindness, goodness, faithfulness, gentleness, and self-control.

— GALATIANS 5:22-23 NLT

The myth of this age is that the human heart produces love. Bundled into this myth is an expectation of peace, joy, kindness, so on and so forth. In actual fact, the spirit-dead human can produce none of these qualities, but instead, produces short-lived emotional replicas.

> "Remain in me [*Jesus Christ*], and I will remain in you. For a branch cannot produce fruit if it is

severed from the vine, and you cannot be fruitful unless you remain in me.

"Yes, I am the vine; you are the branches. Those who remain in me, and I in them, will produce much fruit. For apart from me you can do nothing."

— JOHN 15:4-5 NLT

Expecting fruit from the human heart burdens it with a task it was not designed for. The heart is a muscle that produces *desire,* and so when a person looks to their heart for fruit, the heart compensates by producing the corresponding desire. For example, a woman who seeks to love her friends *from her heart* will find her heart producing a reciprocal need of those friends. Should those needs not be fulfilled, then the corresponding feeling of love will evaporate. True love is a fruit of the spirit, selfless by its very nature, and so needs nothing from the friends in return. True love will not evaporate should the friends not reciprocate.

For people will love only themselves and their money. ... They will be unloving and unforgiving ...

— 2 TIMOTHY 3:2-3 NLT

A heart producing emotional replicas will steadily increase its reciprocal need, a cycle that, when fully developed, becomes an addiction. An addiction can be to a friend's approval, to a chemical intake, to sex, to food. The human heart, of course, has no on-and-off switch, so it will continue to perpetuate the cycle until it destroys the human.

THE FAMILY BOND

A t this point, the keen observer will point out a mother's bond with her child or a wife's goodness to her husband, phenomena prominent even among those who are spirit-dead. How can love like this be possible if the heart is functionally unable to produce love or goodness?

The human heart is, by default, fundamentally selfish. And although a muscle that cannot distinguish between good and bad, the heart can distinguish between its host's body and that of another human. To the mother's heart, her child is a part of her body. And to the child, the mother is a part of his or her body. This is the basis for the bond between them. The mother's heart will produce extraordinary willpower and intentionality on behalf of the child, even to the point of death. The myth of love comes from the fact that the emotion produced within this familial bond is primarily felt as love.

A similar and perhaps more extraordinary phenomenon is at play between a husband and wife. When through the act of sex two people are knit together, the bond is from heart to heart. When this functions correctly and without distortion, each heart will, from that point, see the other person as a part of their person, a part of their body.

> The Lord God caused the man to fall into a deep sleep. While the man slept, the Lord God took out one of the man's ribs and closed up the opening. Then the Lord God made a woman from the rib, and he brought her to the man.
>
> "At last!" the man exclaimed.
> "This one is bone from my bone,
> and flesh from my flesh!
> She will be called 'woman,'
> because she was taken from 'man.'"
>
> This explains why a man leaves his father and mother and is joined to his wife, and the two are united into one.
>
> — GENESIS 2:21-24 NIV

Through this mechanism, then, even without spirit-produced fruit, a heart can produce substantial and powerful instances of *love* and *faithfulness.*

CAPTIVE BY A
CORRUPTED HEART

> For as he thinks in his heart, so is he.

— PROVERBS 23:7 NKJV

Thoughts determine a human's pathway through life. This is most true for thoughts that have their origin in the desires of the heart. Thoughts from the heart are always accompanied by the willpower to seek their reality – they set the trajectory and provide the momentum for a human's life. These *thoughts of the heart* play the largest role in a human's development, transformation, and often destruction.

For this reason, the human heart is on the frontline and bears the brunt of every evil attack.

Once corrupt, a heart has a unique capacity to usurp its host. Spirit-dead and Spiritkind have this in common – it is their heart that provides a home for evil.

> I do not understand what I do. For what I want to do I do not do, but what I hate I do. And if I

do what I do not want to do, I agree that the law is good. As it is, it is no longer I myself who do it, but it is sin living in me. For I know that good itself does not dwell in me, that is, in my sinful nature. For I have the desire to do what is good, but I cannot carry it out. For I do not do the good I want to do, but the evil I do not want to do—this I keep on doing. Now if I do what I do not want to do, it is no longer I who do it, but it is sin living in me that does it.

— ROMANS 7:15-20 NIV

CALLOUSED HEARTS

❧

The human heart is indifferent to the law. It has no prejudice to the moral code, one way or another. What is does intuit, however, is the difference between health and sickness.

That is, until the heart becomes calloused.

> For this people's heart has become calloused;
>   they hardly hear with their ears,
>   and they have closed their eyes.
>   Otherwise they might see with their eyes,
>   hear with their ears,
>   understand with their hearts
>   and turn, and I would heal them.
>
> — MATTHEW 13:15-17 NIV

A calloused heart can no longer see things that are unhealthy for what they are. In an environment saturated with disease, the heart becomes a powerplant for every sinful want. Providing endorphins and dopamine hits for every rebellious activity, the heart is the hapless and fleshly cocon-spirator in the corruption of its host. It simply records each pleasurable outcome, no matter how destructive, then delivers the required willpower for the human to seek it all the more. Every destructive activity becomes a habit, every carnal pleasure becomes an addiction, and suddenly in a vortex of evil, the human is nothing but fuel for the fire.

HARDNESS OF HEART

Callousing is common, but not the only type of 'heart condition.' Another one is *hardness*.

A human who is hard-hearted is inflexible in their intention. They are resolved to a specific course; their *will* is set in stone and they are *unwilling* to make allowances or accommodate others' needs.

This has been a pervasive problem from the very beginning, and an interesting insight into God's perspective on this point came with Moses' law for divorce.

When the law was issued, I can imagine that many in the SUPOX were surprised because it permitted something destructive. The tearing apart of two people knit together by God himself is inherently damaging. But so pervasive is hardness among human hearts, permission for divorce was given on compassionate grounds. When one person is knit together with another whose heart has turned away from them, hardening into a direction by which it will only provide an intentionality to selfish ends, the first person is condemned to a cruel and isolated life. This is the furthest thing from the blessing God intended. Divorce then, was permitted as an act of mercy.

> The Pharisees also came to Him, testing Him, and saying to Him, "Is it lawful for a man to divorce his wife for just any reason?"
>
> And He answered and said to them, "Have you not read that He who made them at the beginning 'made them male and female,' and said, 'For this reason a man shall leave his father and mother and be joined to his wife, and the two shall become one flesh'? So then, they are no longer two but one flesh. Therefore what God has joined together, let not man separate."
>
> They said to Him, "Why then did Moses command to give a certificate of divorce, and to put her away?"
>
> He said to them, "Moses, because of the hardness of your hearts, permitted you to divorce your wives, but from the beginning it was not so. And I say to you, whoever divorces his wife, except for sexual immorality, and marries another, commits adultery; and whoever marries her who is divorced commits adultery."
>
> — MATTHEW 19: 3-9 NKJV

From this, we understand that 'hard-heartedness' has been pervasive from the beginning.

> And He entered the synagogue again, and a man was there who had a withered hand. So they watched Him closely, whether He would heal

him on the Sabbath, so that they might accuse Him. And He said to the man who had the withered hand, "Step forward." Then He said to them, "Is it lawful on the Sabbath to do good or to do evil, to save life or to kill?" But they kept silent. And when He had looked around at them with anger, being grieved by the hardness of their hearts, He said to the man, "Stretch out your hand." And he stretched it out, and his hand was restored as whole as the other. Then the Pharisees went out and immediately plotted with the Herodians against Him, how they might destroy Him.

— MARK 3:1-6 NKJV

A hard heart finds its fatal flaw in this – it is closed off to the single greatest supply of health and provision for any human – God himself. Even being inherently selfish, it is a surprise that the hardened human heart does not recognize the abundant supply that God stands ready to provide. Hardness then has its origins in the seed of rebellion. Once rebellion takes hold, the heart begins to harden, over time slowly closing the door to the Holy Spirit.

Even within a so-called religious person, evidence for the corruption hidden within a hardened heart is in that it will pursue self-sufficiency at all costs. The heart will not recognize God's provision.

> Since they did not know the righteousness of God and sought to establish their own, they did not submit to God's righteousness.

— ROMANS 10:3 NIV

THE GATEWAY FOR
RESURRECTION LIFE

One of them was Lydia from Thyatira, a merchant of expensive purple cloth, who worshiped God. As she listened to us, the Lord opened her heart, and she accepted what Paul was saying.

— ACTS 16:14 NLT

The heart is the gateway for God to enter a spirit-dead human's body. It is the gate by which the immortal joins with the mortal.

And you must love the Lord your God with all your heart, all your soul, and all your strength.

— DEUTERONOMY 6:5 NLT

Through consistent discipline, a heart can be trained to recognize the life-giving sustenance provided by God. Indeed, the heart was designed by God himself to make willpower and intentionality available for the human to open the door to him. By the pathway of the heart the Holy Spirit himself can enter, bringing life, renewal and sustenance.

> "Behold, I stand at the door and knock. If anyone hears My voice and opens the door, I will come in to him and dine with him, and he with Me."
>
> — REVELATION 3:20 NKJV

If a human's heart is open, then there is a pathway for the Holy Spirit.

> Create in me a clean heart, O God,
>   And renew a steadfast spirit within me.
>
> — PSALM 51:10 NKJV

MESSAGE SEEDS AND THOUGHT PLANTS

❦

To complete our understanding of the heart, and prefacing exploration of the mind, we must turn our attention to the nature of messages and thoughts.

"Listen!

A farmer went out to plant some seeds. As he scattered them across his field, some seeds fell on a footpath, and the birds came and ate them. Other seeds fell on shallow soil with underlying rock. The seeds sprouted quickly because the soil was shallow. But the plants soon wilted under the hot sun, and since they didn't have deep roots, they died. Other seeds fell among thorns that grew up and choked out the tender plants. Still other seeds fell on fertile soil, and they produced a crop that was thirty, sixty, and even a hundred times as much as had been planted!

Anyone with ears to hear should listen and understand."

— MATTHEW13:3-9 NLT

Remarkably, the mechanics of what unfolds within us in the SUPOX follows the same laws that can be observed in the natural world around us, our heart and mind operate on the same principles as that of the ecosystem in a forest or field.

Messages, either spoken or written words in the NAPOX, are seeds in the SUPOX. Invisible to the eye in the NAPOX, in the SUPOX they travel from the heart and mind of the speaker to the heart and mind of the receiver.

Thoughts, in a similar way, though invisible in the NAPOX are visible in the SUPOX, a plant-like growth stemming from the seed. Forming part of a person's *nephesh,* they can be seen as they grow from a person's heart into their mind, or vice versa, the exact manifestation of an idea as it grows and develops into decisions and actions. *Thought plants* as we will call them, grow in an almost infinite variety, taking form in keeping with the type of seed from which they sprouted.

From a good message seed sprouts a thought plant that is full of health for the human's body, heart and *nephesh.* Over time, it brings with it various forms of nourishment, healing, and sustenance. Seeds based on the words of God go on to produce plants fundamental to the development of the *nephesh.* They provide the organic fabric, the living fiber for the ever-growing new creation.

A bad seed is the opposite, bringing all forms of harm. Some grow up like a thicket obstructing vision; others are poisonous, abrasive, or thorny. Others entangle the *nephesh* in a strangle-hold.

Now, clearly, I've not seen what I'm talking about in this chapter. I've not observed this in the SUPOX with my own eyes. Where this has been described for us is in the bible – and specifically in Jesus' teaching as quoted at the start of this chapter. Jesus' description of the ecosystem in our heart and mind, be it literal or metaphorical, is a perfect picture and accurate in terms of *function* and *effect*.

> "Now listen to the explanation of the parable about the farmer planting seeds:
>
> The seed that fell on the footpath represents those who hear the message about the Kingdom and don't understand it. Then the evil one comes and snatches away the seed that was planted in their hearts.
>
> The seed on the rocky soil represents those who hear the message and immediately receive it with joy. But since they don't have deep roots, they don't last long. They fall away as soon as they have problems or are persecuted for believing God's word.
>
> The seed that fell among the thorns represents those who hear God's word, but all too quickly the message is crowded out by the worries of this life and the lure of wealth, so no fruit is produced.
>
> The seed that fell on good soil represents those who truly hear and understand God's word and produce a harvest of thirty, sixty, or even a hundred times as much as had been planted!"

— MATTHEW 13:18-23 NLT

What Jesus describes is one specific type of seed and its reception with four different types of people. But it is far more than that. He's describing the inner workings of Mankind - the mechanics he outlines are universal. They are in operation in every single person, at all times, for seeds both good and evil.

Humans can determine which seeds will take root in their hearts – to believe a message is to plant the seed. To believe a good message is to plant a good seed, with a good outcome. To believe a bad message is to plant a bad seed, with a bad outcome.

However, if the person doesn't believe the message, the seed will sit on the surface of the *nephesh* but not germinate. Irrespective of if the seed is good or bad, if the human doesn't believe, then it will not take hold and grow into a thought plant.

> The simple believe anything, but the prudent give thought to their steps.

— PROVERBS 14:15 NIV

> If anyone thinks they are something when they are not, they deceive themselves.

— GALATIANS 6:3 NIV

Thinking and believing something begins the process by which that 'something' will change your life.

As a thought plant puts down roots into a person's *nephesh* it becomes increasingly hard to get out. Ultimately, should the heart start to identify that thought plant as a part of the person, it will do everything it can to protect it. The heart will preserve the plant's hold on the person by withholding the willpower required to remove it.

If the thought plant is that of an evil seed and needs to be uprooted, it will be almost impossible to dislodge with the tools available in the NAPOX. It is only in the SUPOX, and with the power of the Holy Spirit, that the destructive plants that result from evil seeds can be dealt with.

> The weapons we fight with are not the weapons of the world. On the contrary, they have divine power to demolish strongholds. We demolish arguments and every pretension that sets itself up against the knowledge of God, and we take captive every thought to make it obedient to Christ.

— 2 CORINTHIANS 10:4-5 NIV

Let me provide you with a hypothetical. I want you to see the concept of *message seeds* and *thought plants* as it operates in and around us every day, and the easiest way is to follow the life cycle of a bad seed. The seed of a lie. The seed, if you will, of a thought plant *weed*.

Imagine a young girl, let's call her Sally, who has a boyfriend.

He's a handsome lad, and one of Sally's friends spreads the story that this boyfriend has been paying attention to another girl behind Sally's back.

This story, this message, is a seed.

It doesn't matter if it's true or not, it doesn't matter if it's delivered as a scrawled note on a piece of paper or whispered into her ear at lunch. What matters for the purposes of our observation, is if Sally believes it or not.

Does Sally plant the seed?

If, when she hears it she doesn't believe it, it will have no effect on her. It's like the seed has landed on the hard ground. It's unable to take root.

If she does believe it, even if it's days later, she will have given the seed soil to grow. And grow it does, quickly snaking its way downwards into her heart, a nasty line of thinking. The seed has germinated and a brand new *thought plant* has taken hold.

Of course, that's not where the story ends. Thought plants bear fruit, and in the NAPOX, fruit is the actions that result from the thought plant's line of thinking.

The new plant within Sally is a weed, and one of the most potent types. It will be quick to propagate. As a line of thinking it quickly produces symptoms: her demeanor, her mood, and ultimately her response to those around her will now rapidly change. All outcomes in keeping with the nature of the original seed.

So when Sally, flustered and with hands trembling, storms across the playground and slaps her boyfriend sharply across the face, it should come as no surprise. It's completely predictable. The plant has matured and produced a bountiful harvest. It has produced fruit in keeping with its kind.

That's how it works.

> Above all else, guard your heart, for everything you do flows from it.
>
> — PROVERBS 4:23 NIV

Like any garden, there is a caretaker. First and foremost, we are all ourselves responsible for the ecosystem that is our heart and mind.

If Sally, for example, was a little older she might have had the wherewithal to resist immediately believing the message and planting the seed. She could have determined to investigate the truth and taken time to discern the nature of the message. Was it a good seed or bad?

Determining the nature of the seed before allowing it to sink roots into her soul. That would have been a far wiser approach.

And not just to avoid an embarrassing altercation, but to protect the condition of her heart and mind. Allowing such a powerful and destructive plant to take root would undoubtedly produce a tangled mess. If it were true it would be no less painful, but the fruit would be different, perhaps still a bitter pill, but with medicinal qualities in the end.

Managing what you believe and don't believe is the essence of managing your mental self, it is the starting point from which you cultivate the garden of your heart and mind.

Fruit, of course, is the source of more seeds. And as we see in the botanic world of the NAPOX, the process repeats itself. The human *nephesh* is an ever-changing and developing ecosystem; there is no such thing as stasis or equilibrium.

> A troublemaker and a villain,
>> who goes about with a corrupt mouth
>> …
>> who plots evil with deceit in his heart—
>> he always stirs up conflict.
>
> Therefore disaster will overtake him in an instant;
>> he will suddenly be destroyed—without remedy.

— PROVERBS 6:12 & 14-15 NIV

Being a diligent caretaker for the garden of your heart and mind only begins by determining which seed to plant. Once sown, you need to feed, water and nurture anything you want to be healthy. You need to tend to those thought plants in order that they grow and give shape to your life.

> Fix your thoughts on what is true, and honorable, and right, and pure, and lovely, and admirable. Think about things that are excellent and worthy of praise. Keep putting into practice all you learned and received from me—everything you heard from me and saw me doing.

> — PHILIPPIANS 4:8-9 NLT

> May the words of my mouth
> and the meditation of my heart
> be pleasing to you, O Lord

> — PSALM 19:14 NLT

The Gospel, the message about Jesus Christ, is the most important seed of all. It is imperishable, and from it grows a sapling, a tree whose taproot runs deep, drawing up God's very life into a person's innermost parts. The resulting thought plant stands alone among that which grows in the human heart – it is *the tree of life*.

> For you have been born again, not of perishable seed, but of imperishable, through the living and enduring word of God.

> — 1 PETER 1:23 NIV

> Let the message about Christ, in all its richness, fill your lives.

— COLOSSIANS 3:16 NLT

> On the last and greatest day of the festival, Jesus stood and said in a loud voice, "Let anyone who is thirsty come to me and drink. Whoever believes in me, as Scripture has said, rivers of living water will flow from within them." By this he meant the Spirit, whom those who believed in him were later to receive. Up to that time the Spirit had not been given, since Jesus had not yet been glorified.

— JOHN 7:37-39 NIV

THE HUMAN MIND

L̲ike the heart, the mind has form and function in both the NAPOX and the SUPOX. In the former, it is an organ in the body, in the latter it is the nexus of *free will*. Thoughts from the heart arrive in the mind to be combined with a person's free will. It is in the mind they become decisions and then instructions for the body to put into action.

But this is not to say that the mind is the summit of Mankind, or at least, it was not designed to be that way in the beginning. The mind was designed to be subservient to the spirit.

In the global west it is *intellect*, above all else, that is worshiped. Education is hailed a savior, the 'educated' priests at its altar. And, of course, that makes complete sense. For the spirit-dead the mind is all that they're left with. It is the only remaining tower within the ruins of their fallen castle.

Without doubt the mind of mankind is remarkable, but no more remarkable than its Achilles heel. The mind is ultimately subverted by the heart, an inevitable result given that the mind is dependent on *willpower* from the heart to function.

> Those who live according to the flesh have their minds set on what the flesh desires; but those who live in accordance with the Spirit have their minds set on what the Spirit desires. The mind governed by the flesh is death, but the mind governed by the Spirit is life and peace.
>
> — ROMANS 8:5-6 NIV

> Their destiny is destruction, their god is their stomach, and their glory is in their shame. Their mind is set on earthly things.
>
> — PHILIPPIANS 3:19 NIV

The interplay between the heart and the mind is a two-way street.

The most important type of decision a mind can make is that of *belief*. The decision to believe, importantly, is initiated in the mind but then actioned in the heart. Disbelief, equally, is initiated in the mind but then put into effect in the heart. At the instruction of the mind to believe, the heart will allow the corresponding seed associated with the message to take root. At the mind's instruction to disbelieve, the heart will either shun the message seed or, should it already be planted, attempt to uproot it.

There is then an inverse transaction, flowing in the opposite direction.

Beliefs originating in the heart, translate to thoughts in the mind. The heart is not involved in all comings and goings within the mind, many of which pertain only to daily tasks, functions, and bodily directions. But the heart is comprehensively involved in every thought and decision that pertains to God and people. Thoughts of good or evil, these come from the heart.

> "For from the heart come evil thoughts, murder, adultery, all sexual immorality, theft, lying, and slander. These are what defile you."
>
> — MATTHEW 15:19-20 NLT

The thoughts and attitudes of the heart are the substance of a person's *nephesh*. They are the material from which a person's soul and character are formed. They are ultimately what remains of the person when their body passes away, and the sum total of what must then pass through the fire of judgment.

> For the word of God is alive and active. Sharper than any double-edged sword, it penetrates even to dividing soul and spirit, joints and marrow; it judges the thoughts and attitudes of the heart.
>
> — HEBREWS 4:12 NIV

FREE WILL

> The Lord God commanded the man, "You are free..."

— GENESIS 2:16 NIV

We touched in the previous chapter, on a very important subject, that of *free will*. It is worth far more than a passing remark. It is central to every person. It is a gift central to our story.

Into every human is imparted a full measure of *free will*, a gift given to mankind at the beginning. The giving of free will was in many ways a wild gamble – it is a gift that inexorably binds each person to their destiny. Each human's ability, or inability, to wield freedom will ultimately determine their worth.

Let me say that again. It is fundamental to overcoming the web of delusions spun by the devil in these last days.

Your success or failure at wielding freedom will ultimately determine your worth. Your capacity to handle the weight of this profound gift will mark your coming of age.

> The eyes of the Lord search the whole earth in order to strengthen those whose hearts are fully committed to him.

— 2 CHRONICLES 16:9 NLT

> In this all-out match against sin, others have suffered far worse than you, to say nothing of what Jesus went through—all that bloodshed! So don't feel sorry for yourselves. Or have you forgotten how good parents treat children, and that God regards you as his children?

My dear child, don't shrug off God's discipline,
but don't be crushed by it either.
It's the child he loves that he disciplines;
the child he embraces, he also corrects.

God is educating you; that's why you must never drop out. He's treating you as dear children. This trouble you're in isn't punishment; it's training, the normal experience of children. Only irresponsible parents leave children to fend for themselves. Would you prefer an irresponsible God? We respect our own parents for training and not spoiling us, so why not embrace God's training so we can truly live? While we were children, our parents did what seemed best to them. But God is doing what is best for us, training us to live God's holy best. At the time, discipline isn't much fun. It always feels like it's going against the grain. Later, of course, it pays off big-time, for it's the well-trained who find themselves mature in their relationship with God.

— HEBREWS 12:4-11 MSG

God is nothing. That is the lie that is being successfully prosecuted by the world's 'educated'. God is nothing but an idea; *if he does exist, if he is good, why does he not deal with evil?* These clever arguments are the innovation of minds twisted so tight they've severed themselves from reality, as will be seen later in this book. Silently watching, God's eyes roam the earth. Whether we will govern along with Christ in the third age or be fodder for the cleansing flames at the end of the second, what we do with our freedom *now* is the determining factor.

So once again, make sure you understand this. Each person's ability, or inability, to wield freedom will ultimately determine their worth.

It is for this reason, the battle for a person's destiny plays out in their heart and mind.

RESURRECTION AND THE SPLIT OF MANKIND

U sing Version, the devil conquered mankind; he used their decreed dominion, their freedom and free will as a weapon against them. And it was devastating.

Until Christ.

Christ, being injected into dead humanity, effectively split it into two. He split from the original dead-on-their feet Mankind, a new and alive-for-the-first-time, Spiritkind.

How did he achieve this? By what means? It was by that ancient degree that Mankind would always be free to choose. Even though every member of Mankind was spirit-dead, the gift of free will was irrevocable.

> For God's gifts and his call can never be withdrawn.
>
> — ROMANS 11:29 NLT

Activating this ancient law with the resurrection power

of God, Jesus Christ forged a pathway, a pathway from death to life.

> "For just as the Father gives life to those he raises from the dead, so the Son gives life to anyone he wants."
>
> — JOHN 5:21 NLT

He created a gate by which we could pass from death to life, a gate to which we already had the key. *Free will.* All that a person needs to do is plant the seed that comes by the Gospel of Jesus Christ, using the free will they were given at the beginning.

And that's all there is to it. All any human needs to do to activate their transformation from Mankind to Spiritkind, is to believe the message. Within the Gospel of Jesus Christ lies the seed, the imperishable seed of God himself. Believing the message plants the seed in the person's heart, and the Holy Spirit does the rest.

> For you have been born again, not of perishable seed, but of imperishable, through the living and enduring word of God.
>
> — 1 PETER 1:23 NIV

This, though perhaps difficult to comprehend, is the most simple pathway in the world.

TRANSFORMATION AND PROTECTION

❦

> For his Spirit joins with our spirit to affirm that we are God's children.

— ROMANS 8:16 NLT

I n a healthy SpiritKind, the mind is governed by the intermingled Holy Spirit and human spirit. Over time, this governance will completely change how the mind functions, so much so that it becomes capable of operating in the SUPOX, and more specifically, operating in alignment with God.

> Do not conform to the pattern of this world, but be transformed by the renewing of your mind. Then you will be able to test and approve what God's will is—his good, pleasing and perfect will.

— ROMANS 12:2 NIV

Beyond transformation, the spirit also offers the mind protection.

The Holy Spirit helps the human spirit to align with the word of God, and then through prayer and thanksgiving, the flames of the spirit completely envelope the mind. The spirit is the mind's defense, an impervious sheath, effective against anything that would assail it.

> "But when the Father sends the Advocate as my representative—that is, the Holy Spirit—he will teach you everything and will remind you of everything I have told you."
>
> — JOHN 14:26 NLT

> Do not be anxious about anything, but in every situation, by prayer and petition, with thanksgiving, present your requests to God. And the peace of God, which transcends all understanding, will guard your hearts and your minds in Christ Jesus.
>
> — PHILIPPIANS 4:6-7 NIV

THE CONSCIENCE

T he breath of God, imbued into mankind at the very beginning, is still very much alive. It is, I suspect, at the center of every cell that has life. It presents as the person's *conscience,* and functioning something like a compass, it helps Mankind *intuitively* find alignment with God. The conscience is most acutely *felt* in the heart and mind, and allows even those that are spirit-dead to find alignment with his created order, the laws by which every-thing in the NAPOX and SUPOX hold together.

> Indeed, when Gentiles, who do not have the law, do by nature things required by the law, they are a law for themselves, even though they do not have the law. They show that the requirements of the law are written on their hearts, their consciences also bearing witness, and their thoughts sometimes accusing them and at other times even defending them.

— ROMANS 2:14-16 NIV

> When outsiders who have never heard of God's law follow it more or less by instinct, they confirm its truth by their obedience. They show that God's law is not something alien, imposed on us from without, but woven into the very fabric of our creation. There is something deep within them that echoes God's yes and no, right and wrong. Their response to God's yes and no will become public knowledge on the day God makes his final decision about every man and woman.
>
> — ROMANS 2:14-16 MSG

The conscience in its purest form is an excellent guide, and if it were not for the many corrupting influencers working day and night to degrade it, it would almost certainly always bring a wayward person back to God.

I expect the reality is, however, that the compass that is the conscience becomes less and less effective as the fallen feed on the breath of God within a person. These people's consciences become *seared*, more and more ineffective as the life is sucked out from within them.

> The Spirit clearly says that in later times some will abandon the faith and follow deceiving spirits and things taught by demons. Such teachings come through hypocritical liars, whose consciences have been seared as with a hot iron.
>
> — 1 TIMOTHY 4:1-3 NIV

THE GARMENT

W hen the interwoven ecosystem of thoughts stemming from a person's heart and mind extend beyond the frame of their body, it takes the form of a garment and is the person's character. In the SUPOX, this garment is visible, intricate and ever-changing. In my mind's eye it grows upwards and outwards from the heart, wrapping around the person's chest and head and then flowing downwards like a tunic or robe.

> And we all, who with unveiled faces contemplate the Lord's glory, are being transformed into his image with ever-increasing glory, which comes from the Lord, who is the Spirit.
>
> — 2 CORINTHIANS 3:18 NIV

Like a flame to a wick, the luminescent flame of the Spirit hovers just clear of this garment, never touching but never leaving, like a glowing, enveloping flower dancing across the surface. The tongues of flame of the Holy Spirit cause the

God-given elements within the person's garment to glow brighter and brighter, a refining and fulfillment of intended form that takes shape over time. They take on a radiance such that even if not seen, it can be sensed by other humans.

Organic in form, this garment comes as a result of conscious thought and intentional development.

> Therefore put on the whole armor of God, that you may be able to withstand in the evil day, and having done all, to stand. Stand therefore, having the utility belt of truth buckled around your waist, and having put on the breastplate of righteousness, and having fitted your feet with the preparation of the Good News of peace, above all, taking up the shield of faith, with which you will be able to quench all the fiery darts of the evil one. And take the helmet of salvation, and the sword of the Spirit, which is the word of God ...
>
> — EPHESIANS 6:13-17 WEB

Humans that neglect the development of their *nephesh*, their *spiritual selves*, have a garment that resembles something like a drab tangle of weeds, thorns and flake. They have no protection, and the fallen have little trouble sucking out God's breath within them, their very life, even as they still live.

"... you say, 'I am rich, have become wealthy, and have need of nothing'—and do not know that you are wretched, miserable, poor, blind, and naked."

— REVELATION 3:17 NKJV

The final aspect of any garment is that of humility and meekness.

"God blesses those who are humble,
for they will inherit the whole earth."

— MATTHEW 5:5 NLT

Humility presents differently in the SUPOX. Without this intentional covering, humans lose their ability to see as the brightness of their transformation blinds them. Humility can be understood as a robe-like mantle, a drab cloak of concealment by which only the light of the Holy Spirit is visible. The Son of God himself took this cloak when he descended to the dust, and so from that point, it is a great honor for Spiritkind to wear the same.

THE BODY

When created in the beginning, the human body was completely subservient to the spirit. The spirit of Adam with the Spirit of God held a position of supremacy above the *nephesh*, heart, mind and body.

But with the first deception and sin, there was a great inversion. God's Spirit left the man and his own spirit died that same day. From that point, and for all humanity that followed, the heart and mind resumed effective control. In the absence of spirit, flesh ascended the throne. Mankind, from that day forward, became mortal.

But before the inversion the Spirit reigned and the body benefited.

Adam and Eve were immortal.

Adam and Eve's bodies were clothed in the luminescent flame of the spirit.

As their spirits wished, their bodies would follow.

Their bodies, when subservient to the spirit, found no resistance in the NAPOX.

If I may give a most extraordinary example, I imagine that they were fully capable of *transmitting* themselves from place to place. Perhaps this is hard to believe but consider this. That was the recorded nature of the risen Jesus Christ.

Fully human, eating and drinking among them, yet time and time again he would pass through doors, disappear and skip between disciples separated by some distance. He is a picture of what we were. Resurrected, his body returned to its intended position, servant to the spirit.

> Adam, the first man, was made from the dust of the earth, while Christ, the second man, came from heaven. Earthly people are like the earthly man, and heavenly people are like the heavenly man. Just as we are now like the earthly man, we will someday be like the heavenly man.
>
> — 1 CORINTHIANS 15:47-49 NLT

> That Sunday evening the disciples were meeting behind locked doors because they were afraid of the Jewish leaders. Suddenly, Jesus was standing there among them!
>
> ...
>
> Eight days later the disciples were together again, and this time Thomas was with them. The doors were locked; but suddenly, as before, Jesus was standing among them. "Peace be with you," he said.
>
> — JOHN 20:19 & 26 NLT

> Suddenly, their eyes were opened, and they recognized him. And at that moment he disappeared!
>
> ...
>
> Still they stood there in disbelief, filled with joy and wonder. Then he asked them, "Do you have anything here to eat?" They gave him a piece of broiled fish, and he ate it as they watched.

— LUKE 24:31 & 41 NLT

All this, and so much more, is what Adam and Eve at the moment of the first sin, lost in perpetuity. We experience a shadow of this loss when we find ourselves naked in a public place – even the thought of it overwhelms us with a flood of dread and dismay. With the death of their spirit, Adam and Eve found themselves profoundly naked, bare flesh and bone before all that lived in heaven and on earth. Dishonored and disrobed, they had nothing left but a thin membrane of skin and hair. Before animals and angels alike, the crushing shame must have felt like being caught between colliding planets. From that day forward they were spiritually extinguished, no longer a son and daughter of God, nothing but the shell of their former glory.

> I declare to you, brothers and sisters, that flesh and blood cannot inherit the kingdom of God, nor does the perishable inherit the imperishable.

— I CORINTHIANS 15:50 NIV

This separation, separation by death, is what Christ overcame. Christ defeated the force that held that inversion in place. Through Christ every destructive effect of that inversion can be reversed.

> Or don't you know that all of us who were baptized into Christ Jesus were baptized into his death? We were therefore buried with him through baptism into death in order that, just as Christ was raised from the dead through the glory of the Father, we too may live a new life.
>
> ...
>
> For we know that our old self was crucified with him so that the body ruled by sin might be done away with, that we should no longer be slaves to sin— because anyone who has died has been set free from sin.

— ROMANS 6:3-4 & 5-8 NIV

Even the outlandish idea of transmission, now through the power of the Holy Spirit, can be seen among the fringes of Spiritkind.

> He ordered the carriage to stop, and they went down into the water, and Philip baptized him.
>
> When they came up out of the water, the Spirit of the Lord snatched Philip away. The eunuch never saw him again but went on his way rejoicing. Meanwhile, Philip found himself farther north at the town of Azotus. He preached the Good News there and in every town along the way until he came to Caesarea.

— ACTS 8:38-40 NLT

The key to all this, participating in the death of Christ, is something that most Spiritkind never fully achieve until their mortal body is finally destroyed by death itself. But for those that come close, bringing their body into service of the Spirit diminishes the hold of mortal restraints.

> We always carry around in our body the death of Jesus, so that the life of Jesus may also be revealed in our body.
>
> — 2 CORINTHIANS 4:10 NIV

> Now Stephen, a man full of God's grace and power, performed great wonders and signs among the people.
>
> ...
>
> All who were sitting in the Sanhedrin looked intently at Stephen, and they saw that his face was like the face of an angel.
>
> — ACTS 6:8 & 15 NIV

For Spiritkind who never come close to seeing the inversion reversed, the grace of God sees to it that their mortal bodies are sufficient vessels to carry the remarkable gift of his Spirit. And this in itself is no small thing. The Spirit of the ancient and ever-living God held in earthen vessels is a scandalous reversal of Mankind's fate, and to nobody's glory except that of God himself. It is a blinding display of outrageous love, and for the angels who bore witness to this as it unfolded in the first place, it was unthinkable.

> For God, who said, "Let light shine out of darkness," made his light shine in our hearts to give

us the light of the knowledge of God's glory displayed in the face of Christ. But we have this treasure in jars of clay to show that this all-surpassing power is from God and not from us.

— 2 CORINTHIANS 4:6-7 NIV

That night there were shepherds staying in the fields nearby, guarding their flocks of sheep. Suddenly, an angel of the Lord appeared among them, and the radiance of the Lord's glory surrounded them. They were terrified, but the angel reassured them. "Don't be afraid!" he said. "I bring you good news that will bring great joy to all people. The Savior—yes, the Messiah, the Lord—has been born today in Bethlehem, the city of David! And you will recognize him by this sign: You will find a baby wrapped snugly in strips of cloth, lying in a manger."

Suddenly, the angel was joined by a vast host of others—the armies of heaven—praising God and saying,

"Glory to God in highest heaven, and peace on earth to those with whom God is pleased."

— LUKE 2:8-14 NLT

... your body is the temple of the Holy Spirit, who lives in you and was given to you by God ...

1 CORINTHIANS 6:19-20 NLT

The mortal bodies of Spiritkind, when filled with the Holy Spirit, become far more than just a temporary vessel. They themselves become a type of seed, the seed for the body which will be given to the person at the point of resurrection. This new body, subservient to the spirit, will be perfectly at home living both in heaven and on earth, in the NAPOX and the SUPOX, a perfect reflection of Jesus' new heavenly body.

> But someone may ask, "How will the dead be raised? What kind of bodies will they have?" What a foolish question! When you put a seed into the ground, it doesn't grow into a plant unless it dies first. And what you put in the ground is not the plant that will grow, but only a bare seed of wheat or whatever you are planting. Then God gives it the new body he wants it to have. A different plant grows from each kind of seed. Similarly there are different kinds of flesh —one kind for humans, another for animals, another for birds, and another for fish.
>
> There are also bodies in the heavens and bodies on the earth. The glory of the heavenly bodies is different from the glory of the earthly bodies. The sun has one kind of glory, while the moon and stars each have another kind. And even the stars differ from each other in their glory.
>
> It is the same way with the resurrection of the dead. Our earthly bodies are planted in the ground when we die, but they will be raised to live forever. Our bodies are buried in brokenness, but they will be raised in glory. They are buried in weakness, but they will be raised in

strength. They are buried as natural human bodies, but they will be raised as spiritual bodies. For just as there are natural bodies, there are also spiritual bodies.

The Scriptures tell us, "The first man, Adam, became a living person." But the last Adam—that is, Christ—is a life-giving Spirit. What comes first is the natural body, then the spiritual body comes later. Adam, the first man, was made from the dust of the earth, while Christ, the second man, came from heaven. Earthly people are like the earthly man, and heavenly people are like the heavenly man. Just as we are now like the earthly man, we will someday be like the heavenly man.

What I am saying, dear brothers and sisters, is that our physical bodies cannot inherit the Kingdom of God. These dying bodies cannot inherit what will last forever.

But let me reveal to you a wonderful secret. We will not all die, but we will all be transformed! It will happen in a moment, in the blink of an eye, when the last trumpet is blown. For when the trumpet sounds, those who have died will be raised to live forever. And we who are living will also be transformed. For our dying bodies must be transformed into bodies that will never die; our mortal bodies must be transformed into immortal bodies.

Then, when our dying bodies have been transformed into bodies that will never die, this Scripture will be fulfilled:

"Death is swallowed up in victory.
O death, where is your victory?

O death, where is your sting?"

For sin is the sting that results in death, and the law gives sin its power. But thank God! He gives us victory over sin and death through our Lord Jesus Christ.

— 1 CORINTHIANS 15:35-57 NLT

PART V
HISTORY

BEYOND THE HORIZON OF
HUMAN HISTORY

efore we begin this chapter, I think a word of warning is necessary. The exploration and discussion of our place in prophetic history is notorious for causing arguments and ugly division. It is contentious, for the most part, because it involves interpreting scripture's description of the future, for which there is no clear correct interpretation, and the resulting debates are rarely framed with a useful purpose. They become arguments for argument's sake. They become grounds for some to feel superior, and grounds for others to be ostracized. Scripture that was intended for our benefit becomes a tool by which to bludgeon our brothers. I promise you this: I have no such intention.

> Warn them before God against quarreling about words; it is of no value, and only ruins those who listen.

— 2 TIMOTHY 2:14 NIV

Daniel and John, the two witnesses given the task of describing to us the past, the present and the future (in the books now known as Daniel and Revelation), both draw multiple storylines that plot the trajectory of events to and from the arrival and departure of Jesus Christ from the dust. The prophet and the apostle were shown, and subsequently shared with us, our position in history. I believe this was given to us simply so we might more fully understand our calling. I believe the reason they were shown was so we might know who we are.

It is for this reason then that I have written this section. Our position now, in the rocky place between the past and the future, between calamity and resolution, can serve to help us understand *Him* and our relationship to *Him*. Forgive me for any details you see as wrong, bear with me as a brother painting a picture while still mostly blind. Like a man reading braille, I can feel the story written in the pages of scripture, but the color and drama I'm about to describe come only from my mind's eye. My goal in sharing is only this - that you would see Christ *for yourself,* your Messiah in the midst of it all.

> When I first came to you, dear brothers and sisters, I didn't use lofty words and impressive wisdom to tell you God's secret plan. For I decided that while I was with you I would forget everything except Jesus Christ, the one who was crucified. I came to you in weakness—timid and trembling. And my message and my preaching were very plain. Rather than using clever and persuasive speeches, I relied only on the power of the Holy Spirit.

I did this so you would trust not in human wisdom but in the power of God.

— 1 CORINTHIANS 2:1-5 NLT

And so with that context let us begin.

The body of a human, an earthen seed for an immortal body to come, is evidence that we ourselves are at a junction between ages. Born in one, we are destined for the next. But things did not begin with us. The First Age is that of the Angel, the Second Age of Mankind, and the Third Age will be that of Spiritkind, led by Christ himself.

THE FIRST AGE

The First Age is that of the Angel. Lucifer, created as a picture of perfection among them, was himself a Guardian Cherub.

This is what the Sovereign Lord says:
    "'You were the seal of perfection,
    full of wisdom and perfect in beauty.
    …
    You were anointed as a guardian cherub,
    for so I ordained you.
    You were on the holy mount of God;
    you walked among the fiery stones.
    You were blameless in your ways
    from the day you were created
    till wickedness was found in you.

                — EZEKIEL 28:12 & 14-15 NIV

Your heart became proud
    on account of your beauty,

and you corrupted your wisdom
because of your splendor.

— EZEKIEL 28:17 NIV

It was in Lucifer, now known as the Devil, that corruption was first found. Lucifer was the first to conceive and speak Version, an invention that provided the means to fight God on terms close to his own. Lucifer, using Version, would lead a turbulent uprising that would spill violently into the next age.

> "He was a murderer from the beginning. He has always hated the truth, because there is no truth in him. When he lies, it is consistent with his character; for he is a liar and the father of lies."

— JOHN 8:44 NLT

Before Version, Versal was the only power-source for weaponry in the SUPOX. Versal, from God, perfect and pure, gave power, form, and function to every authority in existence. To the shock and dismay of all that lived in heaven, Version changed all that. It was an alternative source of power for weaponry, and in so far as destructive potential, appeared perhaps equal to that of Versal.

By the end of the First Age, Lucifer had consolidated his power in heaven, divided angel against angel, and pitched the created against their Creator. In the midst of this uproar, Lucifer perceived himself as a god, no less than God's equal.

> This is what the Sovereign Lord says:
> "'In the pride of your heart
> you say, "I am a god;

I sit on the throne of a god
in the heart of the seas."

...

"'Because you think you are wise,
as wise as a god,
I am going to bring foreigners against you,
the most ruthless of nations;
they will draw their swords
against your beauty and wisdom
and pierce your shining splendor.
They will bring you down to the pit,
and you will die a violent death
in the heart of the seas.

— EZEKIEL 28:1-2 & 6-8 NIV

Spiritkind, born in the Second Age and foreigners to earth, were to be that nation.

THE SECOND AGE

❧

> In the beginning God created the heavens and the earth. Now the earth was formless and empty, darkness was over the surface of the deep, and the Spirit of God was hovering over the waters.

— GENESIS 1:1-2 NIV

The Second Age is that of Mankind, and its beginning was marked by the creation of the earth. The NAPOX came into form, the visible created by that which is invisible, the qualities of God intrinsic to the SUPOX now visible in a vast and spectacular universe beyond measure.

> For since the creation of the world God's invisible qualities—his eternal power and divine nature—have been clearly seen, being understood from what has been made, so that people are without excuse.

> — ROMANS 1:20 NIV

At the time of Earth's creation, heaven was in turmoil. The corrupted walked alongside the pure, those harboring darkness even among those attending the court of God.

> One day the angels came to present themselves before the Lord, and Satan also came with them. The Lord said to Satan, "Where have you come from?"
>
> Satan answered the Lord, "From roaming throughout the earth, going back and forth on it."

> — JOB 1:6-7 NIV

Earth was perfect in every way, a reflection of its Creator. But as with the fall of Lucifer in the First Age, creation was soon followed by the fall of Mankind in the Second.

At the first sin, and at the death of Father God's dear children, heaven hid their face and held their breath. Who can face the fire of a King whose children are slain, whose younger son and daughter, now spirit-dead, walk disrobed to the shame of the royal family? Though God had rested on the seventh day and heaven celebrated, it seemed now premature. The Father's work was not yet over. At Mankind's rebellion, rather than wrath, he began to speak redemption and resurrection, the final chapter. His plan for the reconciliation of all things, in heaven and on earth, was coming into the world.

These spoken words became visible on the day the Son of God descended into the dust and became the Son of Man, Jesus Christ.

> The Word became flesh and made his dwelling among us. We have seen his glory, the glory of the one and only Son, who came from the Father, full of grace and truth.
>
> — JOHN 1:14 NIV

THE PLAN

B efore this day, however, and indeed for the better part of the Second Age, heaven feared a stalemate. The devil, with mankind hostage and every kind of evil harbored within them, could not be stamped out without massive collateral damage. To eradicate evil would mean the annihilation of Mankind.

But God held in his hand a plan, an impossible but perfect plan to purge heaven and earth of evil. What was missing was this: someone *worthy* to put it into action. No angel, no matter how powerful, was beyond falling like that of their fallen brother Lucifer, formerly the greatest among them. In fact, perhaps the more perfect the more susceptible to such corruption. John, the writer of Revelation, witnessed this and wept at the fate of heaven and earth.

> Then I saw in the right hand of him who sat on the throne a scroll with writing on both sides and sealed with seven seals. And I saw a mighty angel proclaiming in a loud voice, "Who is worthy to break the seals and open the scroll?"

But no one in heaven or on earth or under the earth could open the scroll or even look inside it. I wept and wept because no one was found who was worthy to open the scroll or look inside.

— REVELATION 5:1-4 NIV

Heaven, however, had yet to behold the resurrected Son, the firstborn among the dead. Born a man and in the dusty arms of his human mother given the name Jesus, he was slaughtered as prophesied: the *Passover Lamb*. Returning to his mortal body, he rose from the dead and established the unthinkable - a new Kingdom to rise from among those formerly dead.

> Then one of the elders said to me, "Do not weep! See, the Lion of the tribe of Judah, the Root of David, has triumphed. He is able to open the scroll and its seven seals."
>
> Then I saw a Lamb, looking as if it had been slain, standing at the center of the throne, encircled by the four living creatures and the elders.
>
> ...
>
> And they sang a new song, saying:
> "You are worthy to take the scroll
> and to open its seals,
> because you were slain,
> and with your blood you purchased for God
> persons from every tribe and language
> and people and nation.
> You have made them to be a kingdom
> and priests to serve our God,
> and they will reign on the earth."

— REVELATION 5:5-6 & 9-10 NIV

Jesus, the lamb that was slain, was and became worthy of putting into effect the resolution of all things: executing with perfection a final purge – the eternal eradication of every vestige of evil from heaven and earth.

Jesus Christ, then, would usher in the Third Age. An age that would be ruled by only those who had overcome evil - men and woman born again from the dead. This plan, sealed on the scroll and unsearchable until the ascent of Christ, is the great mystery. The impossible paradox. God's plan would resolve two impossible partners – the perfect preservation of free will, and the permanent eradication of corruption.

Jesus is the pivot on which things now turn.

> I [*Paul*] was chosen to explain to everyone this mysterious plan that God, the Creator of all things, had kept secret from the beginning.
>
> God's purpose in all this was to use the church to display his wisdom in its rich variety to all the unseen rulers and authorities in the heavenly places. This was his eternal plan, which he carried out through Christ Jesus our Lord.

— EPHESIANS 3:9-11 NLT

LUCIFER FORCED FROM HEAVEN

We now rewind the clock to the point that the Son of God first took up mortality, and stood among Mankind on earth. At this point in heaven, the tide was about to turn. Pitching themselves head-first against the devil and his fallen angels, the armies of heaven finally gained the upper hand. Overpowered, he was expelled from the courts of God and thrown from the high place to earth. Unable to return and confined to the dust, earth is where he will take his last stand. Earth then, would become his final fortress.

> Then war broke out in heaven. Michael and his angels fought against the dragon, and the dragon and his angels fought back. But he was not strong enough, and they lost their place in heaven. The great dragon was hurled down— that ancient serpent called the devil, or Satan, who leads the whole world astray. He was hurled to the earth, and his angels with him.
>
> Then I heard a loud voice in heaven say:

"Now have come the salvation and the power
and the kingdom of our God,
and the authority of his Messiah.
For the accuser of our brothers and sisters,
who accuses them before our God
day and night,
has been hurled down.
They triumphed over him
by the blood of the Lamb
and by the word of their testimony;
they did not love their lives so much
as to shrink from death.
Therefore rejoice, you heavens
and you who dwell in them!
But woe to the earth and the sea,
because the devil has gone down to you!
He is filled with fury,
because he knows that his time is short."

— REVELATION 12:7-12 NIV

He [*Jesus*] replied, "I saw Satan fall like lightning from heaven. I have given you authority to trample on snakes and scorpions and to overcome all the power of the enemy; nothing will harm you. However, do not rejoice that the spirits submit to you, but rejoice that your names are written in heaven."

— LUKE 10:18-20 NIV

THE PURGE

❦

> So the Lord God said to the serpent, "Because you have done this,
>> "Cursed are you above all livestock
>> and all wild animals!
>> You will crawl on your belly
>> and you will eat dust
>> all the days of your life.
>> And I will put enmity
>> between you and the woman,
>> and between your offspring and hers;
>> he will crush your head,
>> and you will strike his heel."

— GENESIS 3:14-15 NIV

With the devil thrown to earth, the focus now shifted to the newly resurrected Spiritkind, the church of the Son of God. Cursed to eat dust for the rest of his life, the devil finds himself short on time and facing his greatest enemy: Mankind born anew.

Confined to a realm wholly under the authority of Mankind – he and his angels will not escape when Spiritkind is led against him.

In this battle, Spiritkind will have the chance to prove their worth. They will be by the Son's side in the final battle.

> I saw heaven standing open and there before me was a white horse, whose rider is called Faithful and True. With justice he judges and wages war. His eyes are like blazing fire, and on his head are many crowns. He has a name written on him that no one knows but he himself. He is dressed in a robe dipped in blood, and his name is the Word of God. The armies of heaven were following him, riding on white horses and dressed in fine linen, white and clean. Coming out of his mouth is a sharp sword with which to strike down the nations. "He will rule them with an iron scepter." He treads the winepress of the fury of the wrath of God Almighty. On his robe and on his thigh he has this name written: KING OF KINGS AND LORD OF LORDS.
>
> Then I saw the beast and the kings of the earth and their armies gathered together to wage war against the rider on the horse and his army. But the beast was captured, and with it the false prophet who had performed the signs on its behalf. With these signs he had deluded those who had received the mark of the beast and worshiped its image. The two of them were thrown alive into the fiery lake of burning sulfur.

— REVELATION 19:11-16 & 19-20 NIV

Battle-scarred earth, then, is the stage upon which the Second Age draws to a close. The mystery of the Son's church has been now made clear – those in whom sin has no hold – those who have seen sin put to death inside their own hearts – they will prove themselves worthy of ruling in the Third Age amidst the fire of the battlefield.

> "To all who are victorious, who obey me to the very end,
>
> To them I [Jesus Christ] will give authority over all the nations.
>
> They will rule the nations with an iron rod and smash them like clay pots.
>
> They will have the same authority I received from my Father, and I will also give them the morning star!
>
> Anyone with ears to hear must listen to the Spirit and understand what he is saying to the churches."
>
> — REVELATION 2:26-29 NLT

> And do not grumble, as some of them did—and were killed by the destroying angel. These things happened to them as examples and were written down as warnings for us, on whom the culmination of the ages has come. So, if you think you are standing firm, be careful that you don't fall!
>
> — 1 CORINTHIANS 10:10-12 NIV

And so this is where we find ourselves. It is late in the dark night of the Second Age, facing the imminent dawn of the Third Age. Christ has died and returned not just to life but to heaven for the inauguration.

> He said, "A nobleman was called away to a distant empire to be crowned king and then return. Before he left, he called together ten of his servants and divided among them ten pounds of silver, saying, 'Invest this for me while I am gone.' But his people hated him and sent a delegation after him to say, 'We do not want him to be our king.'
>
> "After he was crowned king, he returned and called in the servants to whom he had given the money.
>
> ...
>
> 'Yes,' the king replied, 'and to those who use well what they are given, even more will be given. But from those who do nothing, even what little they have will be taken away. And as for these enemies of mine who didn't want me to be their king—bring them in and execute them right here in front of me.'"
>
> — LUKE 19:12-15 & 26-27 NLT

This is the hour of tribulation, testing, and judgment — where evil is exposed and prepared for its final destruction. Every vestige of corruption both in heaven and on earth must be dealt with, and will be, with fire.

Among the flames, there will be those among Spiritkind shown as both worthless and worthy. For the latter theirs is a remarkable destiny – the Third Age is theirs and they will rule alongside Christ.

We must each be careful how we build, because Christ is the only foundation. Whatever we build on that foundation will be tested by fire on the day of judgment. Then everyone will find out if we have used gold, silver, and precious stones, or wood, hay, and straw. We will be rewarded if our building is left standing. But if it is destroyed by the fire, we will lose everything. Yet we ourselves will be saved, like someone escaping from flames.

— 1 CORINTHIANS 3:10-13 CEV

After this I looked, and there before me was a great multitude that no one could count, from every nation, tribe, people and language, standing before the throne and before the Lamb. They were wearing white robes and were holding palm branches in their hands.

...

Then one of the elders asked me, "These in white robes—who are they, and where did they come from?" I answered, "Sir, you know." And he said, "These are they who have come out of the great tribulation; they have washed their robes and made them white in the blood of the Lamb.

— REVELATION 7:9 & 13-14 NIV

THE SEATING OF THE COURT

W hat is coming is as shocking as Noah's flood and as final as the fire that fell from heaven on Sodom. For those in whom is found evil, there will be no escape.

God will deal with swift and shocking finality.

> "I have come to bring fire on the earth, and how I wish it were already kindled!

— LUKE 12:49 NIV

> "Just as it was in the days of Noah, so also will it be in the days of the Son of Man. People were eating, drinking, marrying and being given in marriage up to the day Noah entered the ark. Then the flood came and destroyed them all.
>
> "It was the same in the days of Lot. People were eating and drinking, buying and selling, planting and building. But the day Lot left

Sodom, fire and sulfur rained down from heaven and destroyed them all.

"It will be just like this on the day the Son of Man is revealed.

— LUKE 17:26-30 NIV

"I will sweep away everything
    from the face of the earth," says the Lord.
"I will sweep away people and animals alike.
I will sweep away the birds of the sky and the fish in the sea.
I will reduce the wicked to heaps of rubble,
and I will wipe humanity from the face of the earth," says the Lord.

   …

Stand in silence in the presence of the Sovereign Lord,
    for the awesome day of the Lord's judgment is near.
The Lord has prepared his people for a great slaughter
    and has chosen their executioners.

   …

"That terrible day of the Lord is near.
Swiftly it comes—
a day of bitter tears,
a day when even strong men will cry out.
It will be a day when the Lord's anger is poured out—
a day of terrible distress and anguish,
a day of ruin and desolation,
a day of darkness and gloom,
a day of clouds and blackness,

a day of trumpet calls and battle cries.
Down go the walled cities
and the strongest battlements!
"Because you have sinned against the Lord,
I will make you grope around like the blind.
Your blood will be poured into the dust,
and your bodies will lie rotting on the
ground."
Your silver and gold will not save you
on that day of the Lord's anger.
For the whole land will be devoured
by the fire of his jealousy.
He will make a terrifying end
of all the people on earth.

— ZEPHANIAH 1:2-3,7,14-18 NLT

Final destruction comes only after perfect judgment. For this purpose, the judge and jury have assembled. Indeed, judgment has already begun.

During what the world remembers as the World Wars, the court of heaven was assembled. This is no ordinary court, it is the court assigned to preside over and bear witness to the judgment of all. As the judge, God determines the terms of punishment, but as with a court on earth, it is the jury that determines the verdict. Numbering ten thousand times ten thousand, the court of heaven was assembled to preside over those on earth. And delivering the evidence to this immense crowd of jurors would be fire.

Perfect and impartial fire. It would be a fire that reveals the substance hidden within the heart of each and every man. The fire would be the tool by which the truth of all things would be made plain to all.

And so judgment commenced.

As I looked,

> "thrones were set in place,
> and the Ancient of Days took his seat.
> …
> His throne was flaming with fire,
> and its wheels were all ablaze.
> …
> Thousands upon thousands attended him;
> ten thousand times ten thousand stood before him.
> The court was seated,
> and the books were opened.

— DANIEL 7:9-10 NIV

Therefore, since we are surrounded by such a huge crowd of witnesses to the life of faith, let us strip off every weight that slows us down, especially the sin that so easily trips us up.

— HEBREWS 12:1 NLT

"For everyone will be tested with fire."

— MARK 9:49 NLT

This is what is required by the law that the Lord gave Moses: Gold, silver, bronze, iron, tin, lead and anything else that can withstand fire must be put through the fire, and then it will be clean.

— NUMBERS 31:21 NIV

These trials will show that your faith is genuine. It is being tested as fire tests and purifies gold—though your faith is far more precious than mere gold. So when your faith remains strong through many trials, it will bring you much praise and glory and honor on the day when Jesus Christ is revealed to the whole world.

— 1 PETER 1:7 NLT

WORLD WARS

I risk starting an argument with what I'm about to say here, so I will be brief.

I mention the World Wars, that being WWI and WWII, specific moments in history, only to make the case for what was and what is now at this very moment unfolding in heaven outside of what we can see with our mortal eyes. Even if you draw a different conclusion from the scriptures presented, my hope is that you will be convinced of the need to make your remaining days count. That, from this point you will live earnestly, with a sincere heart, knowing you are watched and your words weighed.

Prior to the previously quoted text from Daniel 7:9 the timing of it all is laid out.

From the vantage point of heaven Daniel witnessed the Axis forces, seen in the SUPOX as a beast, an unholy alliance of kingdoms and the first mechanized army of iron ever seen on earth.

> Then in my vision that night, I saw a fourth beast—terrifying, dreadful, and very strong. It

devoured and crushed its victims with huge iron teeth and trampled their remains beneath its feet. It was different from any of the other beasts, and it had ten horns.

As I was looking at the horns, suddenly another small horn appeared among them. Three of the first horns were torn out by the roots to make room for it. This little horn had eyes like human eyes and a mouth that was boasting arrogantly.

I watched as thrones were put in place
and the Ancient One sat down to judge.
His clothing was as white as snow,
his hair like purest wool.
He sat on a fiery throne
with wheels of blazing fire,
and a river of fire was pouring out,
flowing from his presence.
Millions of angels ministered to him;
many millions stood to attend him.
Then the court began its session,
and the books were opened.

I continued to watch because I could hear the little horn's boastful speech. I kept watching until the fourth beast was killed and its body was destroyed by fire. The other three beasts had their authority taken from them, but they were allowed to live a while longer.

As my vision continued that night, I saw someone like a son of man coming with the clouds of heaven. He approached the Ancient One and was led into his presence. He was given authority, honor, and sovereignty over all the nations of the world, so that people of every

race and nation and language would obey him.
His rule is eternal—it will never end. His
kingdom will never be destroyed.

— DANIEL 7:7-14 NLT

Daniel sought an explanation for what he had seen, and
was given this.

> He explained it to me like this:
> "These four huge beasts represent four king-
> doms that will arise from the earth. But in the
> end, the holy people of the Most High will be
> given the kingdom, and they will rule forever
> and ever."
> Then I wanted to know the true meaning of
> the fourth beast, the one so different from the
> others and so terrifying.
> ...
> As I watched, this horn was waging war
> against God's holy people and was defeating
> them, until the Ancient One—the Most High—
> came and judged in favor of his holy people.
> Then the time arrived for the holy people to
> take over the kingdom.
> Then he said to me, "This fourth beast is the
> fourth world power that will rule the earth. It
> will be different from all the others. It will
> devour the whole world, trampling and crushing
> everything in its path. Its ten horns are ten kings
> who will rule that empire. Then another king
> will arise, different from the other ten, who will
> subdue three of them. He will defy the Most
> High and oppress the holy people of the Most

High. He will try to change their sacred festivals and laws, and they will be placed under his control for a time, times, and half a time.

"But then the court will pass judgment, and all his power will be taken away and completely destroyed. Then the sovereignty, power, and greatness of all the kingdoms under heaven will be given to the holy people of the Most High. His kingdom will last forever, and all rulers will serve and obey him."

— DANIEL 7:16-19 & 21-27 NLT

The Axis beast was given the power of life and death over the descendants of Abraham, the Jews, God's people by descent, for the duration of WWII.

> He will defy the Most High and oppress the holy people of the Most High. … they will be placed under his control for a time, times, and half a time.

— DANIEL 7:25 NLT

The judgment and destruction of the Axis beast and the conclusion of the world wars, should they be complete, puts us at the threshold of the third age.

> …the Ancient One—the Most High—came and judged in favor of his holy people. Then the time arrived for the holy people to take over the kingdom.

— DANIEL 7:22 NLT

Daniel's account is corroborated by John in the book of Revelation, and he goes further to add remarkable detail and clarity. Without doubt, there is plenty more to discuss which is beyond the scope of this book, and perhaps my understanding, save one thing: the witness John gave of Christ's final words.

> "Look, I am coming soon! My reward is with me, and I will give to each person according to what they have done. I am the Alpha and the Omega, the First and the Last, the Beginning and the End."
>
> ...
>
> He who testifies to these things says, "Yes, I am coming soon."

— REVELATION 22:12-13 & 20 NLT

THE LAST ALLIANCE

The one detail from John's account we will take a moment to discuss is that of the *image that speaks*, an innovation that has become the foundation of society today.

> Because of the signs it was given power to perform on behalf of the first beast, it deceived the inhabitants of the earth. It ordered them to set up an image in honor of the beast who was wounded by the sword and yet lived. The second beast was given power to give breath to the image of the first beast, so that the image could speak…
>
> — REVELATION 13:14-15 NIV

The first beast, the Axis forces, were struck down in 1919 only to come back to life some twenty short years later. Its miraculous resurrection came while the hapless League of

Nations watched on. They called WWI the *war to end all wars*, but their efforts to entomb the monster that assailed them proved nothing but vanity. The second beast that arose was fiercer than the first, and this one gave breath, gave *speech*, to its image upon the silver screen. What it produced was propaganda, an innovation as famous as those who fashioned and perfected it: the Nazis. What this image-that-speaks has now become, being close to fully grown, is without historical precedent.

The virality of what the beast breathed into it, at the first, is staggering.

The image-that-speaks, every screen of every size and shape, is fast becoming the tool by which all culture takes form. So alluring is its influence and authority, all are attracted to its flickering light. But its stories are duplicitous, and the one whose tongue delicately weaves together the meaning beneath its messages is false.

The image-that-speaks, the screen in all its forms, is of course an innovation of Mankind, and to the casual observer probably has as much to say that is 'good' as it has to say that might be 'bad'. But Version is Versal twisted, it should not be a surprise to find that even the most innocent and whole-some production has an insidious undercurrent, even if those engaged in its production are wholly unaware.

Consider the blockbuster, grand 'save the planet' specta-cles that year after year makes heroes of those who sacrifice themself to save the earth. With their protagonists facing down impossible odds, they hold up sacrifice as the ultimate virtue. They are unoffensive, they contain no swear-words, and many religious folks will go to some lengths to draw parallels between the heroes and their apparent Christ-like qualities. Not a difficult task, as these god-like 'truths' are not just begrudgingly included, they are glamorized.

These 'truths' are eagerly offered up, for the devil is playing bargain, turning what might have been Versal into Version with the stroke of the screenwriter's pen. To Christ, the devil's stories will never bow the knee, but rather their grand aspiration is to call Mankind to an alliance.

The last great alliance.

Saving the planet is, of course, top of the devil's mind. Confined here, trapped in what he knows is a yet-to-be-lit furnace, he and his hordes' very survival rely on mankind's allegiance. Even Spiritkind, if they can play them for the fool.

Not surprisingly, the first films of this kind were made in Nazi Germany. *Kolberg*, shot in the dying days of the war, shines brightest among them, an epic tale of the Prussian town Kolberg's heroic resistance to the last man. Inspiring cinema, it was the ordinary people, not the professional soldiers, who took up arms to repulse the invaders at the cost of their lives. *Kolberg* is looked back upon as propaganda, but that hasn't stopped thousands of other films being made along the same lines. The blockbusters of today are the same, but the war for which they recruit volunteers is hidden just beyond the horizon, a war that is fiction in the mind of Mankind, a biblical legend. Nothing could be further from the truth. The war for which today's blockbusters recruit is none other than Armageddon.

They are demonic spirits who work miracles and go out to all the rulers of the world to gather them for battle against the Lord on that great judgment day of God the Almighty.

"Look, I will come as unexpectedly as a thief! Blessed are all who are watching for me, who keep their clothing ready so they will not have to walk around naked and ashamed."

And the demonic spirits gathered all the rulers and their armies to a place with the Hebrew name Armageddon.

Then the seventh angel poured out his bowl into the air. And a mighty shout came from the throne in the Temple, saying, "It is finished!" Then the thunder crashed and rolled, and lightning flashed. And a great earthquake struck— the worst since people were placed on the earth. The great city of Babylon split into three sections, and the cities of many nations fell into heaps of rubble. So God remembered all of Babylon's sins, and he made her drink the cup that was filled with the wine of his fierce wrath. And every island disappeared, and all the mountains were leveled.

— REVELATION 16:14-20 NLT

Just twenty miles south-west of Jerusalem, burnt a quarter mile into the ground, is the horrible precursor of what is coming. For this was once the land of Sodom and Gomorrah, the beautiful delta of the Jordan River. These sister cities, lying amidst the fertile green, were put to a storm of fire from heaven, a strike from which nothing that lived survived.

Man has forgotten, but the devil has not. All who dwell in the SUPOX know this to be the warning shot. A show of strength such that a million tons of earth went up, vaporized, as a ten-mile-wide pillar of burning sulfur rained down. What remains is a deep scar, the lowest point on earth to this very day. The sea now at the bottom of it, dead. Nothing has or ever will grow there again.

> "...the world will be as it was in the days of Lot. People went about their daily business—eating and drinking, buying and selling, farming and building— until the morning Lot left Sodom. Then fire and burning sulfur rained down from heaven and destroyed them all. Yes, it will be 'business as usual' right up to the day when the Son of Man is revealed."

— LUKE 17:28-30 NLT

To the devil, those who are coming are monsters, bringers of death, harbingers of doom. They are without parallel in all the ages, they are a terror beyond imagination. And in the fight that's coming, he needs Mankind on his side.

So the best filmmakers, the best studios, the best composers and actors are recruited to the cause. The block-buster narrative is simple - defend the planet no matter what, no matter the cost, no matter what assails it. Build mechanized machines, construct weapons, raise the fortress walls. Create monsters such as mankind has never created before: mechs, robots, fighter jets. Whatever it takes. The humans who fight for the preservation of the planet are to be gods, deadly warriors, the heroes on the frontline.

Let's take a breath. Pause here for a minute.

What do we do with this? Say for a second that what I've described is, on the balance of things, correct – what then? Unfortunately, that is something you will have to figure out for yourself. I leave you only with one piece of advice. The image-that-speaks has become the monster in whose shadow we dwell, and so it is far easier to discount these words than to act on them. But, at the end of it all, it is those who overcome the image-that-speaks that will stand.

And I saw what looked like a sea of glass glowing with fire and, standing beside the sea, those who had been victorious over the beast and its image and over the number of its name.

— REVELATION 15:2 NIV

DELUSION AND THE LAWLESS

⧈

> Don't let anyone deceive you in any way, for that
> day will not come until the rebellion occurs and
> the man of lawlessness is revealed, the man
> doomed to destruction. He will oppose and will
> exalt himself over everything that is called God
> or is worshiped, so that he sets himself up in
> God's temple, proclaiming himself to be God.

— 2 THESSALONIANS 2:3-4 NIV

O f the prophetic signposts given to Mankind to
mark the end of the age, the appearance of the
lawless man is possibly the most unexpected.
Like a massive spire hewn from the summit of a distant
mountain, generations of Christians expected to see his
coming at a distance; we imagined that as our path wound
towards the silhouette of his abomination, dark and erect
against a fire-red sky, that we would have all the warning we
would need.

So imagine our astonishment, when one day we awoke to

realize we'd wandered into a valley beset by spires. Not one, but countless smaller ones. Standing side-by-side, row after row, like jagged teeth they lined even the distant valley walls; a vast multitude stretching as far as the eye could see. Enjoying the last of the warm winter sun hanging low in the sky, distracted and preoccupied with our own comfort, we passed through history quicker than expected. We'd not perceived the lengthening of the shadows and not seen what was gathering in them. But that could be forgiven; our most grievous failure was that we'd failed to see what those around us had become.

The lawless man is not just upon us; in many respects, he *is* us.

Those who, in the collective sense, have evolved in their own educated estimation *beyond the need of God,* beyond the natural law of God, are the lawless man. And so here now behold the western man of the 21st century: the man of lawlessness revealed.

> He will oppose and will exalt himself over everything that is called God or is worshiped, so that he sets himself up in God's temple, proclaiming himself to be God. Don't you remember that when I was with you I used to tell you these things?
>
> ...
>
> The coming of the lawless one will be in accordance with how Satan works. He will use all sorts of displays of power through signs and wonders that serve the lie, and all the ways that wickedness deceives those who are perishing.

— 2 THESSALONIANS 2:4-5 & 9-10 NIV

The western man of the 21st century has been crowned with a power never before afforded to Mankind. What the scripture calls *signs and wonders*, the western man calls *technology*. It was given in less than the lifespan of a single man, and it has not passed beyond the memory of the elderly what the world looked like before it came. Life before mankind flew above the birds, before Mankind could create light, before Mankind could rain down fire, death and destruction from the sky. The western man's glory is his technologically enabled magic, and serving its intended illusion, this technology came about by the work of his many collective hands.

Many of you reading this may struggle with what I'm saying. Your career, your life's work, your passion may be this very technology. You may even be using it to further *the work of God*. How can I then call this technology 'power, signs and wonders that serve the lie'? How indeed.

Think of the reality that this technology serves. With that given to him, what empire has western man created? Through his technological signs and wonders, western man has created a world where faith is obsolete. Within his empire, nobody need pray to God. Provision of food is secure, the symptoms of sickness are silenced. Children are conceived on command, their education outsourced, their unruly behavior medicated. You need not fear calamity, there are insurance policies for that.

Pray not to God, but rather submit your request to the help desk. Take a tech-support ticket. Ask not for God's provision, but rather fill in a form for benefits. The empire of the lawless man requires no faith in God.

In the lawless man's empire, your faith, if anywhere, must be in him. Your faith must be in Mankind, a paper-thin portrait of immortal humanity without flaw.

And indeed, there are many reasons to place your faith in

the lawless man. A world of evidence stands ready to reward such confidence. The wonder of the western man's empire is breathtaking, extraordinary in its size and scale.

He has put stars in the heavens, satellites as bright as God's own in the dawn sky. The moon, the ancient and faithful keeper of the night, now hangs dim against dazzling skylines of neon, twinkling yellow, red, pink and blue. Gods and goddesses of sex, fame and fortune effortlessly strut across the sides of buildings, their images clear and 100 meters high, extolling virtues of self-reliance, self-empowerment, and self-actualization. Buy toothpaste for the perfect smile, because *you deserve it*. Deodorant, because you deserve *him*, and he deserves *you*. A credit card, because you deserve *everything*. Stories play over and over again on screens in the home and at cinema alike; Mankind is the hope of the world, the one in whom to have faith. He is the salvation of the planet. Make no mistake, the lawless man of the west is ascending the throne.

> The coming of the lawless one will be in accordance with how Satan works. He will use all sorts of displays of power through signs and wonders that serve the lie, and all the ways that wickedness deceives those who are perishing. They perish because they refused to love the truth and so be saved. For this reason, God sends them a powerful delusion so that they will believe the lie and so that all will be condemned who have not believed the truth but have delighted in wickedness.
>
> — 2 THESSALONIANS 2:9-12 NIV

Again, I take pause for those of you who are reeling at what must seem like outrageous accusations. It's a difficult pill to swallow. Let me slow down and put it in simple terms, as clearly as I can.

I am calling technology 'signs and wonders that serve the lie'. Technology isn't the lie, it serves the lie. Technology, for the most part, has no moral value one way or another, it is neither good nor bad. I've no quarrel with technology. The quarrel I have is with its master. What I'm asserting is that technology in the hands of the ascendant lawless man has *and is* causing the hearts of almost all to fall for the most extraordinary delusion.

And what is the delusion? It is the powerful lie, sent by God, to deceive the perishing. That is the lie that technology has been sent to serve.

The delusion is simply this. That God does not exist.

Never before had such an outrageous hallucination been imagined. Never before had such an egregious deception been so perfectly executed. All of creation, all in heaven and upon earth, from the very beginning through to the very end, declare in the most spectacular terms, the existence of God; larger than the galaxy, generous to a fault and unfailing in faithfulness.

> The heavens proclaim the glory of God.
> The skies display his craftsmanship.
> Day after day they continue to speak;
> night after night they make him known.
> They speak without a sound or word;
> their voice is never heard.
> Yet their message has gone
> throughout the earth,

and their words to all the world.

— PSALM 19:1-4 NLT

Humans, small and frail in an immense and wild world, have always believed in God's existence, even though for the most part they have not have known him. For ten thousand years, the wilderness of the universe has caused those born in the dust to take a knee with respect to God, to he who called forth the stars.

But the people of this new empire are different. Mankind lives in apartments with food, light and water of his own making. He is surrounded only by trinkets of his own design. He travels in a cocoon of comfort, a car, plane or train by which he can hurtle unconfronted through formerly wild-lands now tame. His places of study, work and play are that of glass, plywood and plastic, lifeless but impressive while clean and new. With the confronting largeness of the universe out of sight, the world shrinks until so small he believes it conquered. Perhaps not by himself, but by others like him. He believes in lawless Mankind as God.

Mankind can not so much as bring to life a single blade of grass, duplicate a solitary snowflake or grow healthy hair on a man's bald head, and yet he believes himself as the ultimate, beyond everything that has and ever will be worshipped.

You have been warned. The man of lawlessness is here.

> He will exalt himself and defy everything that people call god and every object of worship. He will even sit in the temple of God, claiming that he himself is God. Don't you remember that I told you about all this when I was with you?

— 2 THESSALONIANS 2:4-5 NLT

The foundation for this delusion pre-dates the coming of the signs and wonders to support it. It was given voice in a modern context by Darwin in 1859; termed *evolution* in the 1870s. When fully developed the idea is that all creation, both living and dead, came from nothing more than a pin-head. Chance is the mother, and time is the father of life itself. Evolution paves the way by which God may be removed from the modern man's mind, and clears the path for the western man to exalt himself over everything that is called God or is worshiped. It is the platform by which the lawless man ascends God's throne, self-declared as the pinnacle of all things in the universe.

Depending on what you've been taught to this point, it may come as a surprise to discover that evidence for evolution remains conspicuously absent, and now 150 years after inception the theory is nothing but a bulging bubble of belief, stretched and distorted out of shape in an effort to remain in place. Only through constant reinflation by the lawless in lab coats does there remain enough hot-air within it to serve the empire on its shoulders.

Don't read into this that I somehow hate science. Far from it - I say follow the scientific process if that is the agreed measuring stick. Evolution is a theory, well enough. Run the experiments to test its presuppositions, collect the data, and put to the fire of reason that which is preached. They teach that life came from a primordial soup, a hot broth of hydroxy- and amino-derivatives such as carbohydrates and proteins. So goes the theory that from this all life sprang. So then, let those in lab coats replicate the phenomena, and become worthy of the title *scientist.* The reality is, given the abundance of life that has presumed to have sprung from nothing, this process should not require a laboratory. If indeed true, and a natural process, then it should be occurring everywhere, all of the time! But if it cannot be replicated and does not occur naturally, then the idea of life coming from nothing must be called for what it is: *not true.* There is no shame for scientists who pursue an honest answer. But their colleagues, who after being denied results for nearly a century, still contest its validity with no new evidence; they have departed the profession. They are no longer worthy of the title *scientist.* Like a judge or a politician with no love for truth, they become a wound for those who listen to them. They are engaged in *fantasy,* they are prosecuting a hoax, they are nothing more than faux-scientists.

So with no lab or scientist able to replicate the emergence of even the tiniest two-cell organism from non-organic matter, the basis for belief sags low. But the lawless in lab coats are unperturbed. Man, in their estimation, is an evolved animal, an ascended ape. Perhaps plausible in its initial 1870s presentation, but now 150 years on, as with the rest of the theory, the evidence that should have been amassed is still missing. Not just is the *missing link* for mankind missing, the link by which every creature under the sun supposedly evolved, is *missing.* Millions by tens of millions of missing links - never found, never so much as seen: the earth is empty of evidence.

The delusion is spectacular.

But it's not the spectacular nature of the delusion that makes it dangerous. Among the perishing, the delusion is loved. Cherished even. As evidenced by the scientist whistle-blowers ousted from the community for calling foul on the evolutionary hoax, it's evidence that lawless man will defend his origin story at any cost. It predicates everything he must believe. *That man himself is god, there is none greater. In all the universe only he can scale the heights of rational thought, only he can be trusted to pilot a course to immortality. The lawless man, Mankind collectively, is god and there are no others.*

It is a delusion profound. Powerful and perfectly executed.

And from on high, God watches. As they whip a frenzy of excitement for the latest device, the newest car, the latest image that can talk, he moves silently among them, listening to the corrupt throb of their hearts, willing that just one might love the truth enough to search for him. But lawless man is in love with himself, and only now beginning to spread his wings of lawless fancy.

Why be bound by the laws of biology? Men can be girls, and women can be boys. The human heart is fundamentally good, so follow it! Why be bound by laws of morality? Have whatever your heart desires! Queen *I can be whatever I want to be* and king *I will do whatever I want to do*, hand in hand, posing as defenders of the downtrodden and saviors of earth, they delight in deceiving each other, and, perishing all the while they will do so till the end.

> The Anarchist's coming is all Satan's work. All his power and signs and miracles are fake, evil sleight of hand that plays to the gallery of those who hate the truth that could save them. And since they're so obsessed with evil, God rubs their noses in it—gives them what they want. Since they refuse to trust truth, they're banished to their chosen world of lies and illusions.
>
> — 2 THESSALONIANS 2:11-12 MSG

It is not fire that brings the fantasy to a bitter finale, but the flashing arrival of majesty and truth from on high.

> ... the man of lawlessness will be revealed, but the Lord Jesus will slay him with the breath of

his mouth and destroy him by the splendor of
his coming.

— 2 THESSALONIANS 2:8 NLT

The fabrication and fallacy will dissolve like a spider web
long dead. The stupidity of it all will blow apart by nothing
more than the appearance of Christ: power and glory
unbridled.

> Woe to those who call evil good
>   and good evil,
>   who put darkness for light
>   and light for darkness,
>   who put bitter for sweet
>   and sweet for bitter.
>   Woe to those who are wise in their own eyes
>   and clever in their own sight.

— ISAIAH 5:20-21 NKJV

FIRES OF FINALITY

The final days of the second age are marked by fire. Fire of all types, from all places, and more than ever before, from millions and millions of human hearts. And you'd never know it. Things in the NAPOX look to be in good order, houses look nice, lawns are well kept, and people drive nice cars. But right around the world the hearts of earth's inhabitants rage. As hate and vitriol sweep across social media, across picket lines and across the dining room table, so fire leaps from one nephesh to the next, a consuming fire-like fury of Mankind's own making.

> "But I promise you that if you are angry with someone, you will have to stand trial. If you call someone a fool, you will be taken to court. And if you say that someone is worthless, you will be in danger of the fires of hell."
>
> — MATTHEW 5:22 CEV

In the SUPOX the air is thick, heavy and hot. Billowing

clouds of smoke and towering dark pillars of ash blot out the sun. And oblivious to it all, keyboard warriors busily demonize their brothers and sisters, spitting fire with every keystroke, slinging hatred with every post. And the *firestorm* approaches. Mankind's collective nephesh, tinder dry and paper thin, is fodder for the furnace, and it will be the words of men that spark the inferno.

> And if one looks at the land,
>> there is only darkness and distress;
>> even the sun will be darkened by clouds.
>
> — ISAIAH 5:30 NIV

> But know this: that in the last days, grievous times will come. For men will be lovers of self, lovers of money, boastful, arrogant, blasphemers, disobedient to parents, unthankful, unholy, without natural affection, unforgiving, slanderers, without self-control, fierce, not lovers of good, traitors, headstrong, conceited, lovers of pleasure rather than lovers of God, holding a form of godliness, but having denied its power.
>
> — 2 TIMOTHY 3:1-5 WEB

> I know, my God, that you test the heart ...
>
> — 1 CHRONICLES 29:17 NIV

For those who hide precious and pure things within their

nephesh, this fire will prove them as worthy. Equally, if a person looks impressive in form but has no substance, this fire will reveal them as naked and destitute.

This is not a season to fear. Everyone must be tested by fire. At a time set in each generation, and especially for those who call themselves the church, there has always been a period of testing. But only those unprepared and those who do not have the Spirit of God, only those need fear such times.

> When you walk through the fire,
>   you will not be burned;
>   the flames will not set you ablaze.
>   For I am the Lord your God,
>   the Holy One of Israel, your Savior;
>   I give Egypt for your ransom,
>   Cush and Seba in your stead.
>
> — ISAIAH 43:2-3 NIV

> Consider it pure joy, my brothers and sisters, whenever you face trials of many kinds, because you know that the testing of your faith produces perseverance. Let perseverance finish its work so that you may be mature and complete, not lacking anything.
>
> — JAMES 1:2-4 NIV

THE THIRD AGE

❧

The Third Age is the age Spiritkind look forward to with eager expectation. It brings with it rest, reward and reconciliation.

It is the age long foretold, an age where evil and corruption no longer hold the balance of power. And it is the age where those resurrected from the dead and proven worthy will rule.

> However, as it is written:
>   "What no eye has seen,
>   what no ear has heard,
>   and what no human mind has conceived"—
>   the things God has prepared for those who love him—
>
> — 1 CORINTHIANS 2:9 NIV

> That power is the same as the mighty strength he exerted when he raised Christ from the dead and seated him at his right hand in the heavenly

realms, far above all rule and authority, power and dominion, and every name that is invoked, not only in the present age but also in the one to come.

— EPHESIANS 1:19-21 NIV

Jesus replied, "The people of this age marry and are given in marriage. But those who are considered worthy of taking part in the age to come and in the resurrection from the dead will neither marry nor be given in marriage, and they can no longer die; for they are like the angels. They are God's children, since they are children of the resurrection.

— LUKE 20:34-36 NIV

Or do you not know that the Lord's people will judge the world? And if you are to judge the world, are you not competent to judge trivial cases? Do you not know that we will judge angels? How much more the things of this life!

— 1 CORINTHIANS 6:2-4 NIV

Amen, Lord. Let it be as you have said.

PART VI
WAR AND WARFARE

THE DEVIL

The devil, formerly Lucifer, was introduced when discussing the First Age in the previous section. He was the picture of perfection, God's finest, and he was appointed to the most important task: guardianship of Mankind.

> You were anointed as a guardian cherub,
> for so I ordained you.

— EZEKIEL 28:14 NIV

Take a moment to contemplate what this means. God assigned the zenith of all created beings to the care of Mankind. But he fell, and Mankind followed him. Don't miss the gravity of what I'm suggesting. For most of human history I suspect we've failed to understand who our adversary is. He is none other than the dark shepherd.

He does not look as you would expect. Not even slightly. Every curse that follows those who fight God and love darkness hangs heavy on his shoulders, that is true. But to those who are perishing he is clothed in a cold but brilliant radiance.

> Satan himself masquerades as an Angel of light.
>
> — 2 CORINTHIANS 11:14 NIV

The devil is the pioneer and inventor of Version, and he stumbles daily upon the sword of this deception. The devil is not immune to his own duplicity.

As you will read in the Annexure that explores the language of lies, Version becomes invisible to those who speak it. Those who speak only Version cannot see the truth. The devil, in the same way, is unable to see his lies as *lies*. He can't discern the deception in that which comes from his own mouth.

> When he lies, he speaks his native language, for he is a liar and the father of lies.
>
> — JOHN 8:44 NIV

Version is the devil's native language, the only language he can speak, hear, understand, and *believe*. It simply means this - the devil has swallowed his own lie. He believes that he is the rightful god of the earth.

The devil believes he is the rightful ruler of both the NAPOX and the SUPOX connected to it. Not just that, but he believes he has gained authority on earth *lawfully*. He believes it so completely that when he confronted the Son of God in the dust of the desert, he felt sure that he would be recognized as the rightful ruler.

> The devil led him [*Jesus*] up to a high place and showed him in an instant all the kingdoms of the world. And he said to him, "I will give you all their authority and splendor; it has been given to me, and I can give it to anyone I want to. If you worship me, it will all be yours."

— LUKE 4:5-7 NIV

The devil presented himself to Jesus as the rightful ruler of earth, and in recognizing Jesus' task, he offered his kingdom to him. Jesus was facing the perfect deception, partly because, more than anything, the devil himself believed it to be true.

Legions of angels had fallen for the delicately poised Version spoken by the devil's silver tongue. But where they fell, Jesus Christ the Son of God, did not.

> Jesus answered, "It is written: 'Worship the Lord your God and serve him only.'"

— LUKE 4:8 NIV

In some way or another, all Mankind had fallen. Every man, woman, and child has bought into one or many of the devil's lies. Version has, universally, been Mankind's undoing. By trading with it, the devil had amassed the authority and splendor of Mankind for himself.

> By your many sins and dishonest trade
>   you have desecrated your sanctuaries.

— EZEKIEL 28:18 NIV

It should come as no surprise then that much of Mankind, especially those given over to religious persuasions, are, in fact, worshiping the devil. The devil believes himself to be God, *as do his followers.*

> You say, "We are wise
>   because we have the teachings
>   and laws of the Lord."
> But I say that your teachers
> have turned my words
> into lies!

— JEREMIAH 8:8 CEV

The devil offers to look after his followers much in the same way God does. He offers to teach them much the same way God does. On the surface, it looks almost the same. Only when peeling back the scab to look beneath the surface does the horror become apparent. While feeding his followers self-importance, pride, and power, the devil feeds on them. Each draws strength from the other, an alluring exchange that leads his disciples on a treacherous descent into depravity.

> Lies come from the mouths
>   of my people,
>   like arrows from a bow.
> With each dishonest deed
> their power increases…

— JEREMIAH 9:3 CEV

> Look at that man, bloated by self-importance—
> full of himself but soul-empty.

— HABAKKUK 2:4 MSG

> Now the Spirit expressly says that in latter times
> some will depart from the faith, giving heed to
> deceiving spirits and doctrines of demons,
> speaking lies in hypocrisy, having their own
> conscience seared with a hot iron, forbidding to
> marry, and commanding to abstain from foods
> which God created to be received with thanks-
> giving by those who believe and know the
> truth.

— 1 TIMOTHY 4:1-3 NKJV

> Dear friends, do not believe every spirit, but test
> the spirits to see whether they are from God,
> because many false prophets have gone out into
> the world.

— 1 JOHN 4:1 NIV

The devil feeding on his followers, remarkably, does nothing to sap his followers' devotion. So passionate were these devil-god followers in Jesus' time they desired murder above all else. Not for any reason except this – Jesus called them out. Christ not only unmasked their false religion, but he called out their god as the devil. He disrobed him, removing his radiant and god-like mask of deception.

> "If you were Abraham's children," said Jesus,
> "then you would do what Abraham did. As it is,

you are looking for a way to kill me, a man who has told you the truth that I heard from God. Abraham did not do such things. You are doing the works of your own father."

"We are not illegitimate children," they protested. "The only Father we have is God himself."

Jesus said to them, "If God were your Father, you would love me, for I have come here from God. I have not come on my own; God sent me. Why is my language not clear to you? Because you are unable to hear what I say. You belong to your father, the devil, and you want to carry out your father's desires. He was a murderer from the beginning, not holding to the truth, for there is no truth in him. When he lies, he speaks his native language, for he is a liar and the father of lies. Yet because I tell the truth, you do not believe me!

— JOHN 8:39-45 NIV

The devil, then, is the god of this age. Except for Spiritkind, his worshipers one and all, have gone after him.

> Anyone with ears to hear
> should listen and understand.
> Anyone who is destined for prison
> will be taken to prison.
> Anyone destined to die by the sword
> will die by the sword.
> This means that God's holy people must endure persecution patiently and remain faithful.

— REVELATION 13:9-10 NLT

FALLEN ANGELS

"God presides over heaven's court;
   he pronounces judgment on the heavenly
beings:
   "How long will you hand down unjust
decisions
   by favoring the wicked? Interlude
   "Give justice to the poor and the orphan;
   uphold the rights of the oppressed and the
destitute.
   Rescue the poor and helpless;
   deliver them from the grasp of evil people.
   But these oppressors know nothing;
   they are so ignorant!
   They wander about in darkness,
   while the whole world is shaken to the core.
   I say, 'You are gods;
   you are all children of the Most High.
   But you will die like mere mortals

and fall like every other ruler.'"

— PSALM 82:1-7 NLT

F allen angels are former shepherds who now feed on the very flock they were assigned to care for.

…angels are only servants—spirits sent to care for people who will inherit salvation.

— HEBREWS 1:14 NLT

"What sorrow awaits the leaders of my people— the shepherds of my sheep—for they have destroyed and scattered the very ones they were expected to care for," says the Lord.

— JEREMIAH 23:1 NLT

Originally given to the earth as servants of Mankind, they have become tyrants, intended to be a blessing, now they bring nothing but death.

The nature of fallen angels is not spoken of much in the scriptures. However, we can draw conclusions based on the similarities between them and the spirit-dead of Mankind, a parallel established in Jude, the second-to-last book of the bible.

…the angels who did not keep their positions of authority but abandoned their proper dwelling—these he has kept in darkness, bound with everlasting chains for judgment on the great Day. In a similar way, Sodom and Gomorrah and the surrounding towns gave themselves up to sexual immorality and perversion...

...

these people slander whatever they do not understand, and the very things they do understand by instinct—as irrational animals do—will destroy them.

Woe to them! They have taken the way of Cain; they have rushed for profit into Balaam's error; they have been destroyed in Korah's rebellion.

These people are blemishes at your love feasts, eating with you without the slightest qualm—shepherds who feed only themselves. They are clouds without rain, blown along by the wind; autumn trees, without fruit and uprooted—twice dead. They are wild waves of the sea, foaming up their shame; wandering stars, for whom blackest darkness has been reserved forever.

— JUDE 1:6-7 & 10-13 NIV

Separated from the life of God, the fallen are like degraded animals, their senses dulled and their functionality reduced to instinct. What they do is irrational; they are savagely pursuing their own destruction. No longer looking like the angels they once were, they go by a new name – the demon.

They slander that which they do not understand: Jesus Christ, his Church, the Holy Spirit and the gift of grace. They are voracious. They wound, poison, and infect with disease.

They tangle their prey with cords of guilt and shame to keep them compliant. They feast on the vulnerable.

But they are not only fixated on killing that which has God's favor. Led by the devil, the fallen *favor the wicked*, trading with any man who is willing, offering rewards for sin. For acts of rebellion they offer bursts of wealth and success, such is theirs to offer, bounty that comes to a bitter end.

Trading offers a form of legitimacy. Via transactions, humans both explicitly and implicitly grant the fallen permission to dwell in the SUPOX, feed on their *nephesh*, and control earth.

The fallen are twice dead. Fruitless - having shrunk back from paying the price to be everything God created them to be. Severed - forever separated from the life of God.

They have seen the very face of God and yet turned: there is no grace for these.

> ... if we deliberately continue sinning after we have received knowledge of the truth, there is no longer any sacrifice that will cover these sins. There is only the terrible expectation of God's judgment and the raging fire ...
>
> ... I will take no pleasure in anyone who turns away."
>
> But we are not like those who turn away from God to their own destruction. We are the faithful ones, whose souls will be saved.

— HEBREWS 10:26-27 & 38-39 NLT

> They will go from one place to another, weary and hungry. And because they are hungry, they will rage and curse their king and their God.

They will look up to heaven and down at the earth, but wherever they look, there will be trouble and anguish and dark despair. They will be thrown out into the darkness.

— ISAIAH 8:21-22 NLT

The fallen are wandering stars, homeless, and with no future. There is no salvation. There is no redemption. Theirs is a horrible end.

GUARDIAN ANGELS

uardian Angels serve God and Jesus Christ, working to support the Holy Spirit's ministry among Spiritkind. They are given tasks of protection and intervention.

They are no longer given the responsibility of teaching and guidance. Since Christ became firstborn among the dead, Spiritkind is exclusively in the care of the Holy Spirit, the Spirit of Jesus Christ himself.

> "...be sure of this: I am with you always, even to the end of the age."
>
> — MATTHEW 28:20 NLT

Let me say it again and emphasize the point. Cultivation, fostering the fruit of the Spirit and planting seeds that correlate with the Word of God is not a task assigned to angels. This is singularly the task of the Father, the Son and the Holy Spirit.

> "I am the true vine, and My Father is the vine-dresser. Every branch in Me that does not bear fruit He takes away; and every branch that bears fruit He prunes, that it may bear more fruit. You are already clean because of the word which I have spoken to you. Abide in Me, and I in you. As the branch cannot bear fruit of itself, unless it abides in the vine, neither can you, unless you abide in Me."

— JOHN 15:1-4 NKJV

Although angels had been tasked with delivering messages and instruction to Mankind in years gone by, it is not something that they're well suited for. When compared to the Holy Spirit, this is especially apparent - the Spirit's union and communion with Spiritkind is like a glove to a hand; it is perfect by design and was intended that way from the very beginning.

> … God revealed these things by his Spirit. For his Spirit searches out everything and shows us God's deep secrets. No one can know a person's thoughts except that person's own spirit, and no one can know God's thoughts except God's own Spirit. And we have received God's Spirit (not the world's spirit), so we can know the wonderful things God has freely given us.
>
> When we tell you these things, we do not use words that come from human wisdom. Instead, we speak words given to us by the Spirit, using the Spirit's words to explain spiritual truths. But people who aren't spiritual can't receive these truths from God's Spirit. It all sounds foolish to

them and they can't understand it, for only those who are spiritual can understand what the Spirit means.

— 1 CORINTHIANS 2:10-14 NLT

But the law was designed to last only until the coming of the child who was promised. God gave his law through angels to Moses, who was the mediator between God and the people.

— GALATIANS 3:19 NLT

"But you are not to be called 'Rabbi,' for you have one Teacher, and you are all brothers. And do not call anyone on earth 'father,' for you have one Father, and he is in heaven. Nor are you to be called instructors, for you have one Instructor, the Messiah."

— MATTHEW 23:8-10 NIV

Angels wage war with Versal, the Word of God, facing off against their fallen brethren who wield opposing weapons of Version, the language of the devil.

Guardian Angels serve Christ. They surround and protect the humans in their care not just to help them survive, but to see their revival and foster their own capacity to fight. When Spiritkind fights it is the Guardian Angel who fights alongside them.

I have not seen angels, and so I am unable to tell you anything other than what I read in the bible. So it's from the pages of scripture that I imagine the Guardian Angels' final task is to ensure their human always has a way to escape temptation.

> No temptation has overtaken you except what is common to mankind. And God is faithful; he will not let you be tempted beyond what you can bear. But when you are tempted, he will also provide a way out so that you can endure it.
>
> — 1 CORINTHIANS 10:13 NIV

CAN A GUARDIAN ANGEL FALL?

A Guardian Angel, like any other angel, can fall. They are not immune to that which deceived those who have already joined Lucifer's rebellion.

How can it happen? And what can we learn from it? As I've said before, and to avoid any illusions about what I'm sharing, I've not seen angels. What I share comes from the common ground that angels share with humans, the commonality that stems from shared servanthood.

> I [John] fell down to worship at the feet of the angel who showed them to me. But he said, "No, don't worship me. I am a servant of God, just like you and your brothers the prophets, as well as all who obey what is written in this book. Worship only God!"
>
> — REVELATION 22:8-9 NLT

The first and most lethal way for an angel to fall likely comes in the heat of battle. Should an angel twist the word of

God and fashion a weapon of Version, no matter how desperate the moment, they wring the neck of their own umbilical cord. In an instant they pierce their connection to the life of God that radiates through them.

> A fool's mouth lashes out with pride,
> but the lips of the wise protect them.
>
> — PROVERBS 14:3 NIV

> The words of the reckless pierce like swords,
> but the tongue of the wise brings healing.
>
> — PROVERBS 12:18 NIV

> But even the archangel Michael, when he was disputing with the devil about the body of Moses, did not himself dare to condemn him for slander but said, "The Lord rebuke you!" Yet these people slander whatever they do not understand, and the very things they do understand by instinct—as irrational animals do—will destroy them.
>
> — JUDE 1:9-10 NIV

Fashioning a weapon of Version, twisting Versal to create a weapon, even if as a last resort and to achieve a righteous goal, cuts their connection to God and seals their fate.

There was an angel who took leave of God to do exactly this, and although often overlooked it is one of the most extraordinary accounts in the bible.

> Then Micaiah said, "Therefore hear the word of the Lord:
>
> I saw the Lord sitting on His throne, and all the host of heaven standing by, on His right hand and on His left. And the Lord said, 'Who will persuade Ahab to go up, that he may fall at Ramoth Gilead?' So one spoke in this manner, and another spoke in that manner.
>
> Then a spirit came forward and stood before the Lord, and said, 'I will persuade him.' The Lord said to him, 'In what way?' So he said, 'I will go out and be a lying spirit in the mouth of all his prophets.' And the Lord said, 'You shall persuade him, and also prevail. Go out and do so.'
>
> Therefore look! The Lord has put a lying spirit in the mouth of all these prophets of yours, and the Lord has declared disaster against you."

— 1 KINGS 22:19-23 NKJV

Perhaps you think that the angel in this account returned to God's court having achieved the given task. I doubt it. Jesus Christ gave Judas leave in much the same way, and Judas, departing his presence would never return.

> Now after the piece of bread, Satan entered him. Then Jesus said to him, "What you do, do quickly."
>
> ...

Having received the piece of bread, he then went out immediately. And it was night.

— JOHN 13:27 & 30 NKJV

Piercing his own master for love of money, Judas departed the company of life never to return. Surely to speak Version is like drawing a ragged razor across one's throat.

Guardians who find themselves in a pitched battle with their fallen brethren quickly learn there is no honor in the fight. Their tactics are well enough seen in the spirit-dead that fight for them - they fight not just to crush those who oppose them, but if they can, cause them to join their ranks.

> "You travel over land and sea to win a single convert, and when you have succeeded, you make them twice as much a child of hell as you are."

— MATTHEW 23:15 NIV

> Furthermore, just as they did not think it worthwhile to retain the knowledge of God, so God gave them over to a depraved mind, so that they do what ought not to be done. They have become filled with every kind of wickedness, evil, greed and depravity.
>
> ...
>
> Although they know God's righteous decree that those who do such things deserve death, they not only continue to do these very things but also approve of those who practice them.

— ROMANS 1:28-29 & 32 NIV

The second way a Guardian can fall is by accepting human worship. Being worshiped isn't on the angel's head, but accepting such worship is. I suspect this is one reason why angels avoid detection at all costs in the NAPOX.

> At this I fell at his feet to worship him. But he said to me, "Don't do that! I am a fellow servant with you and with your brothers and sisters who hold to the testimony of Jesus. Worship God! For it is the Spirit of prophecy who bears testimony to Jesus."

— REVELATION 19:10 NIV

The third way a Guardian can fall is by accepting counsel from a fallen angel. It perhaps seems like an impossible scenario but consider this. A fallen angel who can see their mistake may appear to possess a form of wisdom - that they might be able to teach others from the folly of their fall. But any such pretense has an insidious deception woven through it, for they are dead and no wisdom is to be found within them. For this reason, anyone who engages in conversation with a forlorn, a dead angel, is in treacherous territory.

> Someone may say to you, "Let's ask the mediums and those who consult the spirits of the dead. With their whisperings and mutterings, they will tell us what to do." But shouldn't people ask God for guidance? Should the living seek guidance from the dead?
> Look to God's instructions and teachings! People who contradict his word are completely in the dark. They will go from one place to another, weary and hungry. And because they

are hungry, they will rage and curse their king and their God. They will look up to heaven and down at the earth, but wherever they look, there will be trouble and anguish and dark despair. They will be thrown out into the darkness.

— ISAIAH 8:19-22 NLT

The last snare by which an angel can fall is hidden, I suspect, in specifically how they relate to men. Angels are no longer tasked with providing instruction or wisdom to humans, unless given voice by the Spirit himself, as stated by the angel in Revelation 19 quoted above, *"For it is the Spirit of prophecy who bears testimony to Jesus."* God's Spirit, the Spirit of prophecy, can infill Spiritkind and angel alike, but outside this, for an angel to assume a position of teaching and authority over any human is to dangerously overstep the mark. They would be stepping into a role reserved for Jesus Christ and the Holy Spirit, and if an angel were to do so, they would cross the threshold into fatal territory.

"When the Spirit of truth comes, he will guide you into all truth. He will not speak on his own but will tell you what he has heard. He will tell you about the future. He will bring me [Jesus Christ] glory by telling you whatever he receives from me. All that belongs to the Father is mine; this is why I said, 'The Spirit will tell you whatever he receives from me.'"

— JOHN 16:13-16 NLT

Dear friends, do not believe every spirit, but test the spirits to see whether they are from God, because many false prophets have gone out into the world. This is how you can recognize the Spirit of God: Every spirit that acknowledges that Jesus Christ has come in the flesh is from God, but every spirit that does not acknowledge Jesus is not from God. This is the spirit of the antichrist, which you have heard is coming and even now is already in the world.

— 1 JOHN 4:1-3 NIV

If an angel whispers instruction into the mind of a human, even for what might be at the outset a righteous cause, they have departed from service – they have exalted themselves above Christ.

Both the human and the angel will realize their folly when they discover the spirit cannot acknowledge Christ as God and from God.

It's hard to understand how a Guardian Angel would make such a mistake, and if they were deceived to somehow make an error, why they would not immediately repent and return to God. The reality is, for those who have beheld God's glory and received the truth, there is no excuse. To return is to face an infinitely searing heat – the fiery wrath of God's presence.

It is on impulse, a base instinct even, that once fallen they find themselves, like Adam, suddenly seeking darkness to conceal their deeds.

"Everyone who does evil hates the light, and will not come into the light for fear that their deeds will be exposed."

— JOHN 3:20 NIV

" Dear friends, if we deliberately continue sinning after we have received knowledge of the truth, there is no longer any sacrifice that will cover these sins. There is only the terrible expectation of God's judgment and the raging fire that will consume his enemies. For anyone who refused to obey the law of Moses was put to death without mercy on the testimony of two or three witnesses. Just think how much worse the punishment will be for those who have trampled on the Son of God, and have treated the blood of the covenant, which made us holy, as if it were common and unholy, and have insulted and disdained the Holy Spirit who brings God's mercy to us. For we know the one who said,

"I will take revenge.

I will pay them back."

He also said,

"The Lord will judge his own people."

It is a terrible thing to fall into the hands of the living God.

— HEBREWS 10:26-31 NLT

WEAPONS OF WARFARE

I n the SUPOX, although the weapons used by angels and their fallen brethren look entirely different, there are two aspects in which they are virtually identical.

Firstly, weapons used in the SUPOX draw their power from words. Words, both of Versal and Version, are the power source behind every weapon.

> The tongue has the power of life and death,
>   and those who love it will eat its fruit.

— PROVERBS 18:21 NIV

> At evening they return,
>   They growl like a dog,
>   And go all around the city.
>   Indeed, they belch with their mouth;
>   Swords are in their lips;
>   For they say, "Who hears?"

— PSALM 59:7 NKJV

The second similarity in the weapons of angels and demons is that their weapon's effectiveness is determined by *authority*. Not just their authority, but the authority of the person who speaks the words that power the weapon. Words spoken by humans in the NAPOX power the weapons of those in the SUPOX. Although a person cannot see what's unfolding, they can feel the heat of a battle exploding in conjunction with a verbal tirade, be it one they're giving or receiving, for good or bad. They are speaking into the air, power for weaponry in the SUPOX.

> For though we live in the world, we do not wage war as the world does. The weapons we fight with are not the weapons of the world. On the contrary, they have divine power to demolish strongholds. We demolish arguments and every pretension that sets itself up against the knowledge of God, and we take captive every thought to make it obedient to Christ.
>
> — 2 CORINTHIANS 10:3-5 NIV

> Whoever loves a quarrel loves sin …
>
> — PROVERBS 17:19 NIV

For the authority that a human holds, they themselves can become the fallen angel's greatest asset. The fallen have only improvised weapons, a shadow of what they had before they fell. But when Version is used to harness a human, they can wield the person's words and authority in a dark symphony to devastating effect. If they can create a puppet of the person, they become a formidable opponent. A weaponized human hostage is something of an army tank in SUPOX warfare.

The fallen, indeed the devil himself, has a perverted sense of righteousness when doing this to their victims. Believing that they are gods themselves, and knowing that God fashions his own servants as weapons, they see themselves as acting righteously and within the authority they've acquired.

> And He [*the Lord*] has made My mouth like a sharp sword;
> In the shadow of His hand He has hidden Me,
> And made Me a polished shaft;
> In His quiver He has hidden Me."
>
> — ISAIAH 49:2 NKJV

This is where the similarities between the weapons of angels and fallen angels end.

WEAPONS OF ANGELS AND DEMONS

❧

L et me be frank. Angels are real, their weapons are real and their battles are real. Their reality is often relegated to fantasy by those who worship their western education, but that doesn't take away from their weight of existence. I say this, because, although a good deal of the color and detail I'm about to describe is akin to fiction, you can see for yourself in clear enough detail, that the bible presents the weapons used in the SUPOX as fact.

> So He drove out the man; and He placed cherubim at the east of the garden of Eden, and a flaming sword which turned every way, to guard the way to the tree of life.

— GENESIS 3:24 NKJV

The weapons wielded by angels have but one source. They draw their power and form from Versal, God's spoken word. Rendered a straight-edged sword, it is a means by which they bring into effect the *will of God* with precision and deadly finality.

> .. take the sword of the Spirit, which is the word of God.

— EPHESIANS 6:17 NLT

> Then the angel said, "I am Gabriel! I stand in the very presence of God. It was he who sent me to bring you this good news! But now, since you didn't believe what I said, you will be silent and unable to speak until the child is born.

— LUKE 1:19-20 NLT

> Then the Lord opened Balaam's eyes, and he saw the Angel of the Lord standing in the way with His drawn sword in His hand; and he bowed his head and fell flat on his face. And the Angel of the Lord said to him, "Why have you struck your donkey these three times? Behold, I have come out to stand against you, because your way is perverse before Me. The donkey saw Me and turned aside from Me these three times. If she had not turned aside from Me, surely I would also have killed you by now, and let her live."

— NUMBERS 22:31-33 NKJV

> And the people kept shouting, "The voice of a god and not of a man!" Then immediately an angel of the Lord struck him, because he did not

give glory to God. And he was eaten by worms and died.

— ACTS 12:22-23 NKJV

I imagine when a Guardian Angel receives their commission they are given their own unique hilt, specifically crafted for them. It is a symbol signifying their authority to wield the words of God on God's behalf. An angel, taking the hilt in two hands, holds it to the side of their face, and speaks the words given to them by the Spirit. The words materialize as flashes of white light suspended in the air, and as the angel draws the hilt backwards they fill out the form of the blade, joining the hilt when fully extended. The words are now in weaponized form – flashing white-hot and double-edged.

> When I turned to see who was speaking to me ... standing in the middle of the lampstands was someone like the Son of Man. ... He held seven stars in his right hand, and a sharp two-edged sword came from his mouth.
>
> — REVELATION 1:12-13 & 16 NLT

> Therefore I cut you in pieces with my prophets,
>   I killed you with the words of my mouth—
> then my judgments go forth like the sun.
>
> — HOSEA 6:5 NIV

> The unfolding of your words gives light ...
>
> — PSALM 119:130 NIV

A blade like this is not just for battle, but being formed of Versal, the very word of God, it provides piercing illumination. Not just to angels, but as we will see in the next section, also to Spiritkind.

> The commands of the Lord are radiant,
> giving light to the eyes.

— PSALM 19:8 NIV

With the light from the weaponized word of God, angels can see clearly through the tangled web of deception spun by the enemy. What was set to ensnare becomes as smoke and dissolves, the enemy painfully illuminated by its light. Held to its blade, a fallen angel can neither run nor hide.

Weapons of Versal are not found among the fallen. A fallen angel cannot breathe God's words into form; no blade will come from their hilt. Rather, they must use their hilt to pull a weapon from within themselves. God's word, twisted into Version in their gut, produces a weapon ridden with bile and poison.

A crude but effective implement somewhat like a curved scimitar with a jagged blade, it is a manifestation of stating something that is not as though it is. It takes little imagination to see that forming a weapon of Version is in and of itself rebellion.

Cutting, distorting and twisting Versal out of shape within themselves, they permanently and irrevocably amputate their connection to God. Just as was the case with Adam- they die on the day they create their first weapon. Forming a weapon of Version is how an angel becomes a demon.

> Woe to those who call evil good

and good evil,
who put darkness for light
and light for darkness,
who put bitter for sweet
and sweet for bitter.
Woe to those who are wise in their own eyes
and clever in their own sight.

— ISAIAH 5:20-21 NKJV

The most effective weapons are smoothed with saliva, easing the weapon's passing as it enters the human *nephesh*.

> The words of his mouth were smoother than butter,
> But war was in his heart;
> His words were softer than oil,
> Yet they were drawn swords.

— PSALM 55:21 NKJV

By improvising and modifying their hilt, fallen angels have been able to produce different weapons, producing weapons in keeping with their particular perversion of choice.

Universally, however, the weapons fashioned for use against humans are crafted to effect *control.*

> We know that we are children of God, and that the whole world is under the control of the evil one.

— 1 JOHN 5:19 NIV

Take a harpoon-styled weapon, for example. A barbed shaft attached to a cord, once thrust into a human, allows the fallen angel to tug at the person, lurching them to the right and the left. A group of the fallen can use these weapons to manipulate a person like a puppet.

> Woe to those who draw sin along with cords of deceit, and wickedness as with cart ropes
>
> — ISAIAH 5:18 NIV

> When tempted, no one should say, "God is tempting me." For God cannot be tempted by evil, nor does he tempt anyone; but each person is tempted when they are dragged away by their own evil desire and enticed.
>
> — JAMES 1:13-14 NIV

As fearsome as these implements are, however, they are not the most dangerous among those available to a demon. The most grievous weapon, by any measure, is a complicit human.

A human, controlled through cords of deceit, and with their own weapons of Version in hand, can inflict incalculable damage in both the NAPOX and the SUPOX. It was by these weapons the prophets were killed. It was by these weapons that the Israelites were ensnared of old. It is by these weapons that generations have been led to the slaughter. And it was by these weapons that the Christ himself was tortured and killed.

> The wicked watches the righteous,

And seeks to slay him.

— PSALM 37:32 NKJV

For the lips of an immoral woman drip honey,
    And her mouth is smoother than oil;
    But in the end she is bitter as wormwood,
    Sharp as a two-edged sword.
    Her feet go down to death,
    Her steps lay hold of hell.

— PROVERBS 5:3-5 NKJV

My child, if sinners entice you,
    turn your back on them!
    They may say, "Come and join us.
    Let's hide and kill someone!
    Just for fun, let's ambush the innocent!
    Let's swallow them alive, like the grave;
    let's swallow them whole, like those who go
down to the pit of death.

— PROVERBS 1:10-12 NLT

The weaponized human is an accomplice in the harvesting of people upon whom the demon can feed.

Will those who do evil never learn?
    They eat up my people like bread
    and wouldn't think of praying to the Lord.

— PSALM 14:4 NLT

Shocking though the suggestion might be, I think you

will know it well enough from experience. There is a transaction that takes place that cannot be explained in the natural. Take, for example, an instance when you are bullied. Be it at work, home or at school, irrespective of who the perpetrator is and context for when the bullying occurs, there is almost universally an extraction of *life* from within you. This emotional deficit makes very little sense when assessed by only what you can see in the NAPOX. You might even be critical of yourself, feeling that you are to blame for being so thin-skinned. But think on what is happening *inside*. Your courage is sapped, your zest for life is sucked from your bones, your enthusiasm – completely drained. Physically you are fine, the picture of health even. But for you the world turns grey, you feel sick to the core.

You, my friend, are being fed upon.

The person who is bullying you is just the weapon. Although they draw some strength from serving their master, they are not the recipient of the life that is leaving you. Not in the slightest. Your life, the life that God gave you from the beginning, is being consumed by that which hides in the bully's shadow. Though the perpetrator likely has no idea, they have been weaponized. Weaponized and set to work on you.

There are any number of scriptures I could present to illustrate this in action, but rather I want to point our attention to just one, the words of a man who could see both sides of the equation with complete clarity.

> When they came to a place called The Skull, they nailed him to the cross. And the criminals were also crucified—one on his right and one on his left.
>
> Jesus said, "Father, forgive them, for they don't know what they are doing." And the

soldiers gambled for his clothes by throwing dice.

— LUKE 23:33-34 NLT

It is necessary at this point to make a short but decisive detour. There will be those who, having read to this point, now feel strongly obliged to do humanity a great favor: head down the street and burn to the ground the houses of those who willingly delight in being a weapon of the enemy.

Do not do that.

It's been done before, so much so it's a cliché complete with pitchforks and torches. By this even those who were once the church have been co-opted into devil-led campaigns for power, dominion and blood. Fire cannot be quenched with fire. Should you try, you will find the demon that hid in the shadow of your enemy now residing in your own. It has played this game before, pitting neighbor against neighbor since the beginning. I counsel you: calm down, stay your desire for justice, wait on God.

> ... do not avenge yourselves, but *rather* give place to wrath; for it is written, "Vengeance *is* Mine, I will repay," says the Lord.

— ROMANS 12:19 NKJV

> But the people of the village did not welcome Jesus because he was on his way to Jerusalem. When James and John saw this, they said to Jesus, "Lord, should we call down fire from heaven to burn them up?"

But Jesus turned and rebuked them.

— LUKE 9:53-55 NLT

> Jesus turned to Peter and said, "Get away from me, Satan! You are a dangerous trap to me. You are seeing things merely from a human point of view, not from God's."

— MATTHEW 16:23 NLT

The devil is both the pioneer of weapons powered by Version and the architect of his own godless empire. In pursuit of complete control, his most potent weapon is the *ruephush.*

> … above all, taking up the shield of faith, with which you will be able to quench all the fiery darts of the evil one.

— EPHESIANS 6:16 WEB

Resembling a delicate flower, the *ruephush* looks nothing like a weapon. Thousands of tiny, barbed darts held together in a perfectly symmetrical sphere, they materialize on the tip of his tongue like a dandelion. As he breathes the darts take flight, filling the air in slowly spiraling circles, now flickering with flame. Penetrating almost everything, they are perfectly designed to tightly lodge in the human nephesh.

Although effective at close range, these weapons possess no capacity to project their effect at a distance. To achieve any kind of effect at scale they need human technology. And as it turns out, in the final years of the second age, mankind has been more than willing to oblige.

These dart-like fire seeds are perfectly adapted for systems of human design: innovations for mass communication. *Images that speak.* They duplicate and deliver deception en mass. In this way the devil's *ruephush* has become his ultimate weapon, the key to a universal and global empire.

Even so, the devil still requires co-opted humans to outwork his plans, and so in every generation sets about finding a selected few who have the requisite gifts he can co-opt to deceive the masses. Adolf Hitler was just one of these.

As touched on previously, the transmission of grand scale lies was first weaponized by the Nazis as *propaganda*. But this pioneering of the *silver screen*, the 'image that can speak,' was really nothing more than a field test. Even Hitler and Goebbels never imagined the scale at which their work would be applied. The future forming in the mind of the devil was one where the entire world would have an *image that speaks* in the palm of their hand.

And as the world crossed into the third millennium, the *ruephesh* was combined with the internet. Self-replicating and incredibly virulent, this new confederation began spinning vast webs of deception faster and faster, almost now approaching the speed of light. Death, on the wings of 400Mbs fiber-optic connections. Foreign to the fallen at inception, this product of the devil's diseased innovative mind was a tool of ultimate rebellion, an apparatus capable of seeding infection in everything it touched. The co-opting and corruption of information itself. News. Fake news. Porn. False importance. Distraction. Death. Death porn, death news, death itself. An explosion of distracting idols at the fingertips of the idle: sports, fitness, health, weather, fame and fortune, all carrying the dandelion seeds of lies of the *ruephush*. It was like biological warfare, the corruption of all things that exist, mass corruption of an entire generation's *nephesh*, and then setting them all collectively alight.

Don't be deceived. This is the precipice upon which we stand, even as you read these words.

The devil's destructive potential takes your breath away. But he is not nearly as impressive as the destruction that awaits him, and as the clock runs out the noose around his neck draws ever tighter.

There is nothing that the devil invents that can cause God injury, and there is nothing the devil invents that can separate Spiritkind from God's love. God's impartation of immortality is untouchable.

The devil is, and always will be, fighting a losing battle.

> "See, it is I who created the blacksmith
> who fans the coals into flame
> and forges a weapon fit for its work.
> And it is I who have created the destroyer to wreak havoc;
> no weapon forged against you will prevail,
> and you will refute every tongue that accuses you.
> This is the heritage of the servants of the Lord,
> and this is their vindication from me,"
> declares the Lord.

— ISAIAH 54:16-17 NIV

SPIRITKIND WEAPONS

The final type of weapon is wielded by Spiritkind.

It is a wild and fearsome thing for angelic beings to behold for one simple reason - the weapon Spiritkind wields in the SUPOX is the most potent there is.

When in synchronization with the Holy Spirit, the words of God spoken by Spiritkind produce a weapon that is similar in form to that of the angel, but with one striking difference: Spiritkind require no hilt. They have been given authority to wield the words of God as sons of God. Indeed, from the beginning they were designed to wield such a weapon naturally. I imagine it as a blade that envelops the person's forearms and extends out before them, not one but two sharp and flashing white double-edged swords.

These are the swords of the Spirit.

> In truthful speech and in the power of God; with weapons of righteousness in the right hand and in the left
>
> — 2 CORINTHIANS 6:7 NIV

> And take the helmet of salvation, and the sword of the Spirit, which is the word of God;
>
> — EPHESIANS 6:17 WEB

It is organic in form, changing with the intention that the words are spoken. And not just spoken but sung, shouted and roared. Invoked from the mouths of a few or of many, it is a powerful and *living* weapon.

The sword of the Spirit invokes something of the Holy Spirit's omnipresence. When in use through prayer, Spiritkind are not bound to their physical location in the NAPOX but can temporarily project the use of their weapon to another location in the SUPOX, wielding the blades as if there themselves.

> Even though I [*Paul*] am not with you in person, I am with you in the Spirit. And as though I were there, I have already passed judgment on this man in the name of the Lord Jesus. You must call a meeting of the church. I will be present with you in spirit, and so will the power of our Lord Jesus.
>
> — 1 CORINTHIANS 5:3-5 NLT

> I [*Paul*] want you to know how hard I am contending for you and for those at Laodicea,

and for all who have not met me personally. ... For though I am absent from you in body, I am present with you in spirit and delight to see how disciplined you are and how firm your faith in Christ is.

— COLOSSIANS 2:1&5 NIV

At the location of their projection, their weapon appears in full strength, and behind it an apparition of their own form. By this means, Spiritkind can amass a great army almost instantly, anywhere, a possibility that terrifies the fallen. Against such attacks, even against just a handful, the devil has no defense.

"Assuredly, I say to you, whatever you bind on earth will be bound in heaven, and whatever you loose on earth will be loosed in heaven.

"Again I say to you that if two of you agree on earth concerning anything that they ask, it will be done for them by My Father in heaven."

— MATTHEW 18:18-19 NKJV

If you remain in me and my words remain in you, ask whatever you wish, and it will be done for you.

— JOHN 15:7 NIV

And we are confident that he hears us whenever we ask for anything that pleases him. And since we know he hears us when we make our requests, we also know that he will give us what we ask for.

— 1 JOHN 5:14-15 NLT

It is a picture of Spiritkind's full, collective potential. Captained by Christ himself, this phenomenon is a picture of what will unfold in the Third Age.

> Together they will go to war against the Lamb, but the Lamb will defeat them because he is Lord of all lords and King of all kings. And his called and chosen and faithful ones will be with him."

— REVELATION 17:14 NLT

THE BATTLE GROUND

The battleground in the SUPOX of the earth has little in common with military operations as we know them. If a comparison must be drawn, it perhaps resembles a resurgence within already occupied enemy territory, an uprising or a resistance.

The Kingdom of God, the kingdom built by Christ and the Holy Spirit of Spiritkind, was established *within* an already long-established empire - the devil's earthen empire of the fallen. In and of itself, the devil's empire is a confederation of territories controlled by powerful fallen angels, an alliance of powers in the SUPOX that somewhat resembles the patchwork of nations in the visible NAPOX. Surrounding them all, figuratively speaking, are walls of death and the gates of Hades.

When Jesus Christ brought the Kingdom of God into being, he made a declaration. He declared that death would not be able to restrain his church, Spiritkind. Against their advance the gates of Hades would hold no power.

It was a declaration of war.

> Simon Peter answered, "You are the Messiah, the Son of the living God." Jesus replied, "Blessed are you, Simon son of Jonah, for this was not revealed to you by flesh and blood, but by my Father in heaven. And I tell you that you are Peter, and on this rock I will build my church, and the gates of Hades will not overcome it.

— MATTHEW 16:16-18 NIV

Since the resurrection of Christ and his ascension to heaven, the new Kingdom has been viciously and continually attacked. It has been assaulted on every side, but inexplicably, never defeated. Even when pushed to the brink of oblivion, it has survived. And more than that, it has steadily prevailed. In a war waged for over two thousand years the Kingdom of God has taken ground in every country, among every people, even to the ends of the earth.

> But we have this treasure in jars of clay to show that this all-surpassing power is from God and not from us. We are hard pressed on every side, but not crushed; perplexed, but not in despair; persecuted, but not abandoned; struck down, but not destroyed.

— 2 CORINTHIANS 4:7-9 NIV

It is not a military success like we see among earth's nations. There are no flags fluttering from the turrets, no grand parades, no soldiers returning to confetti and streamers. Success, rather, is marked with peace, with a quiet humility and with the restoration of things long broken.

Centuries before, King Nebuchadnezzar was shown the inexplicable nature of this new Kingdom, and Daniel gave meaning to his vision.

> In the time of those kings, the God of heaven will set up a kingdom that will never be destroyed, nor will it be left to another people. It will crush all those kingdoms and bring them to an end, but it will itself endure forever. This is the meaning of the vision of the rock cut out of a mountain, but not by human hands—a rock that broke the iron, the bronze, the clay, the silver and the gold to pieces.
>
> "The great God has shown the king what will take place in the future. The dream is true and its interpretation is trustworthy."
>
> — DANIEL 2:44-45 NIV

Today, approaching the end of the Second Age, there is fighting on every front. Right across the global west the enemy is on the move. In some places there are great bursts of light amidst intense darkness, but these victories are against a bleak backdrop. Over the top of once liberated territory, great storm clouds have gathered. Once great fortresses of Spiritkind lay under siege, their defensive lines overrun in all directions. Losses are heavy, and the wounded have turned on their brothers and sisters. There are enemies inside the camp, wolves among the sheep. But in the developing world, indeed in overlooked Africa, there the enemy is on the back foot. Vast swathes of territory are taken every day, with the dark rulers and authorities in full retreat. Ancient strongholds that have stood firm since the beginning are now falling.

> For our wrestling is not against flesh and blood,
> but against the principalities, against the
> powers, against the world's rulers of the dark-
> ness of this age, and against the spiritual forces
> of wickedness in the heavenly places.

— EPHESIANS 6:12 WEB

Amidst all of this, on every front, there is carnage in the streets.

The fallen can still manipulate Spiritkind much the same way they can with the spirit-dead. The ill-prepared, imma-ture and apathetic are an easy target. Even so, it's not a demon's first choice: the luminescent flame of the Holy Spirit causes their rotting flesh to burn. But driven in rage and consumed by a hatred of God and all that's dear to him, if Spiritkind makes themselves vulnerable, then they will even at great cost attack and feed.

> I say this because many deceivers, who do not
> acknowledge Jesus Christ as coming in the flesh,
> have gone out into the world. Any such person
> is the deceiver and the antichrist. Watch out that
> you do not lose what we have worked for, but
> that you may be rewarded fully. Anyone who
> runs ahead and does not continue in the
> teaching of Christ does not have God; whoever
> continues in the teaching has both the Father
> and the Son. If anyone comes to you and does
> not bring this teaching, do not take them into
> your house or welcome them. Anyone who
> welcomes them shares in their wicked work.

— 2 JOHN 7-11 NIV

In this fight, Spiritkind are not alone.

At the command of Christ, angels defend and protect. Standing against enemies both in the NAPOX and the SUPOX an angel will position themselves between their charge and the hostile force. For children weak and blind, this protection is given at great cost, it is hard to imagine that the angel does so without great risk to themselves.

> Because you have made Yahweh your refuge,
> and the Most High your dwelling place,
> no evil shall happen to you,
> neither shall any plague come near your dwelling.
> For he will put his angels in charge of you,
> to guard you in all your ways.
> They will bear you up in their hands,
> so that you won't dash your foot against a stone.
> You will tread on the lion and cobra.
> You will trample the young lion and the serpent underfoot.
>
> — PSALM 91:9-13 WEB

The protection of angels, however, does not guarantee an outcome. The fate of the person does not rest in a Guardian Angel's hands. How their charge uses the gift of *free will* is what sets the person's trajectory. Whether or not the person determines to make God their dwelling is the determining factor.

Because of this, there is no certainty of success in a fight between guardians and the fallen.

CONTEST FOR CONTROL

Angels and demons in the earthern SUPOX fight for mankind. These battles unfold within the bounds of God's law, much in the same way that earth's military commanders must successfully navigate natural forces of wind and water to be successful. Beyond that, and most importantly, battles unfold according to the various levels of authority held and assigned by humans. For the better part of the Second Age, the fact that large tracts of human authority had been handed over to the devil gave the fallen a home-town advantage; they held all the cards.

That is until Jesus Christ and the rebirth of Spiritkind from among men. The appearance of Spiritkind on the battlefield completely changed the game.

> "I [*Jesus Christ*] will give you the keys of the kingdom of heaven; whatever you bind on earth will be bound in heaven, and whatever you loose on earth will be loosed in heaven."
>
> — MATTHEW 16:19 NIV

> When the seventy-two disciples returned, they joyfully reported to him, "Lord, even the demons obey us when we use your name!"
>
> — LUKE 10:17 NLT

In this chapter I want to turn our attention to those battles that unfold outside the influence of Spiritkind. Many of the battles that Guardian Angels face are for a person yet to be born of the Spirit, or still an infant. The person must mature before they have any chance of effectively using their authority in the SUPOX for themselves, but that does not mean they don't have a hand in the outcome of a fight for their life.

In so far as a Guardian Angel and his fallen angel adversary are concerned, the fight for this person will be Versal versus Version. And it is the human, the person over which the angel and demon fight, that through accepting or rejecting deception will determine the result. They may be none the wiser as to what is unfolding in the SUPOX, but are nevertheless integral to the outcome.

To understand this, remember that Mankind, both the spirit-dead and Spiritkind collectively, have been given dominion. Breaking down beneath this are sub-levels of God-assigned authority. Authority in government, authority in the home, authority over the body, heart and soul.

> For the husband is the head of the wife as Christ is the head of the church, his body, of which he is the Savior.
>
> — EPHESIANS 5:23 NIV

> Husbands, in the same way be considerate as you live with your wives, and treat them with respect as the weaker partner and as heirs with you of the gracious gift of life, so that nothing will hinder your prayers.

> — 1 PETER 3:7 NIV

> Consequently, whoever rebels against the authority is rebelling against what God has instituted, and those who do so will bring judgment on themselves.
>
> ...
>
> For the one in authority is God's servant for your good.
>
> ...
>
> Give to everyone what you owe them: If you owe taxes, pay taxes; if revenue, then revenue; if respect, then respect; if honor, then honor.

> — ROMANS 13:2, 4 & 7 NIV

For example, imagine a family scenario, with the father as the head and the mother as the head under the father. Should a father be of the mind to intercede for his son, and the son accepts it, it carries tremendous weight in the SUPOX. If the son unwittingly had granted a demon access through believing a lie the demon planted, but the father rejected its claim, then the demon would be without authority. With access revoked, and if he could not stir up the son to reject the father's authority, the demon would have to leave.

Should the mother either intentionally or unwittingly grant a demon access over a daughter, but the daughter rejects it, then it's contentious territory. The daughter is under the authority of the mother and so in this instance, mercy comes into play.

If, by the prayers of the daughter, an angel assigned by God contends with the demon on the grounds of authority, it will be an ugly fight. Invoking God's mercy for the daughter, the angel may gain the upper hand, break the deadlock and protect the girl. Prayers by an aunty or grandmother may well also be a factor that tips the scales in favor of the daughter. As you will remember, authority is granted *collectively*.

Under no circumstances, even if they wanted, can an angel or a demon find a way to be effective without God or the human's consent. On earth, authority is in Mankind's collective hands. It is division among Mankind, all forms of infighting, insubordination, derision and defiance that produce the cracks through which the fallen can take advantage.

> "Every kingdom divided against itself will be ruined, and every city or household divided against itself will not stand"

> — MATTHEW 12:25 NIV

GRANTING AUTHORITY BY
INFERENCE

 ⁂

onsent, the assignment of Authority, can be implied. With Mankind, who for the most part is unaware of the SUPOX, this happens all the time. Let me give you an example. When a human disconnects from God's life, 'breaking God's law,' and removes themselves from the provision and blessing that flows as a result, a demon can argue the human is intentionally choosing death. The decision is implied, even if it is not deliberate.

> But those who fail to find me [*wisdom*] harm themselves;
>   all who hate me love death."
>
> — PROVERBS 8:36 NIV

An angel can defend the human for a time, calling into effect God's grace to cover the indiscretion, but only for a time, and only if they're already there. God's grace is without limit, but a man's decision must be respected. Ultimately, then, the consequences of this implied decision will be brought to bear, and the angel will be forced to withdraw.

This happens in many instances with the human none the wiser. Awaking one day to find their life in pieces, their soul sapped of strength, and their best years gone, they wonder what on earth happened. And, of course, nothing *on earth* happened. It all unfolded in the SUPOX.

> "When an impure spirit comes out of a person, it goes through arid places seeking rest and does not find it. Then it says, 'I will return to the house I left.' When it arrives, it finds the house unoccupied, swept clean and put in order. Then it goes and takes with it seven other spirits more wicked than itself, and they go in and live there. And the final condition of that person is worse than the first. That is how it will be with this wicked generation."
>
> — MATTHEW 12:43-45 NIV

Unattended and abandoned, mankind has become the hideout for a host of demons. Earth became home for the fallen, the last fortress of evil in defiance of God.

PART VII
THE SON

JESUS CHRIST, THE SON OF GOD, THE MESSIAH

> "I am the Alpha and the Omega, the First and the Last, the Beginning and the End."
>
> — REVELATION 22:13 NIV

Here at last, we arrive at the crux of it all. We come to fully face the Son of God, the man named Jesus Christ, the most supremely important piece of the puzzle, the beginning and the end of *everything*.

Knowledge of Jesus Christ is necessary to perceive our place in history, but that knowledge in and of itself is only the surface, nothing more than the superficial beginning. What I will share with you in this simple chapter, a mere thousand words or so, carries within its words a seed. Though unseen, this seed is the key to the germination within yourself of the life I have explained in this book. This seed has the capacity to open your eyes, not to see my crude descriptions, but to see the truth of them, the reality of an invisible Kingdom. It is by this seed that you are born of the Holy Spirit.

> "I tell you the truth, unless you are born again,
> you cannot see the Kingdom of God."
>
> — JOHN 3:3 NLT

At the end of it all, an intimate and personal trust in Jesus Christ is the key to unlocking a wild transformation within every human being. It confers to the person an ability to pass from death to life, from being spirit-dead to being Spiritkind.

Who then is Jesus Christ the Messiah?

He was not always known as Jesus Christ. Before he descended to the dust to join the ranks of Mankind, he was known as the Son or the Word, one third of the Godhead, along with God the Father and the Holy Spirit.

> In the beginning the Word already existed.
> > The Word was with God,
> > and the Word was God.
> > He existed in the beginning with God.
> > God created everything through him,
> > and nothing was created except through him.
> > The Word gave life
> > to everything that was created,
> > and his life brought light to everyone.
>
> — JOHN 1:1-4 NLT

> In the past God spoke to our ancestors through
> the prophets at many times and in various ways,
> but in these last days he has spoken to us by his
> Son, whom he appointed heir of all things, and

through whom also he made the universe. The Son is the radiance of God's glory and the exact representation of his being, sustaining all things by his powerful word. After he had provided purification for sins, he sat down at the right hand of the Majesty in heaven.

— HEBREWS 1:1-3 NIV

The Son of God is and has always been.

He is the one through whom the universe was made.

He is the origin, the substance, and sustainer of Versal, and through Versal, he caused all things that are to take form.

He is not just the substance and exact representation of God, he is the firstborn among the dead.

> The Son is the image of the invisible God, the firstborn over all creation. For in him all things were created: things in heaven and on earth, visible and invisible, whether thrones or powers or rulers or authorities; all things have been created through him and for him. He is before all things, and in him all things hold together. And he is the head of the body, the church; he is the beginning and the firstborn from among the dead, so that in everything he might have the supremacy.

— COLOSSIANS 1:15-18 NIV

And so here begins his story.

In the beginning, the Son was the same in nature as God: omnipresent, everywhere all at once, and omnipotent, all-powerful. The Son was the Word of God. To put it another way, he was the radiance of God. Everything of God was transmitted via the Son.

> In the beginning was the Word, and the Word was with God, and the Word was God. He was with God in the beginning. Through him all things were made; without him nothing was made that has been made. In him was life, and that life was the light of all mankind.
>
> — JOHN 1:1-4 NIV

Through this radiance, this transmission, this Word, everything in both heaven and earth was given form and function. All things that are alive have life from God through the Son. It is for this reason he is known as the *Word of God.*

> The Son is the radiance of God's glory and the exact representation of his being, sustaining all things by his powerful word.
>
> — HEBREWS 1:2-3 NIV

> … hear, O earth, the words of my mouth.
> Let my teaching drop as the rain,
> My speech distill as the dew,
> As raindrops on the tender herb,
> And as showers on the grass.
>
> — DEUTERONOMY 32:1 NKJV

Begotten of God, Mankind was as a second-born son, and

had complete and intimate fellowship with God the Father. But Mankind fell.

The fall of man and then the subsequent introduction of the written law put Mankind into a form of stasis. Incapable of putting down the rebellion within them and insatiably in love with death, their intended destiny was put on hold. *Indefinitely.* They would have to wait until the rebellion, Version and the power that undergirds it, had been dealt with.

By their own doing, and for this reason, Mankind was put under the care of 'guardians and trustees'.

The Son was not among these guardians and trustees, but instead, angels were appointed along with God's law. Among those given this assignment were angels who remained pure, those who had fallen, and those who had yet to fall.

> But I say that so long as the heir is a child, he is no different from a bondservant, though he is lord of all, but is under guardians and stewards until the day appointed by the father. So we also, when we were children, were held in bondage under the elemental principles of the world. But when the fullness of the time came, God sent out his Son, born to a woman, born under the law, that he might redeem those who were under the law, that we might receive the adoption as children.
>
> And because you are children, God sent out the Spirit of his Son into your hearts, crying, "Abba, Father!" So you are no longer a bondservant, but a son; and if a son, then an heir of God through Christ.
>
> However at that time, not knowing God, you

were in bondage to those who by nature are not gods. But now that you have come to know God, or rather to be known by God, why do you turn back again to the weak and miserable elemental principles, to which you desire to be in bondage all over again?

— GALATIANS 4:1-9 WEB

Mankind then was under the law, and by the law their love of death was illuminated. Its black stain like a leprous decay, they were shown as dead; even that which was alive was being eaten. By the law of God the sin of rebellion among fallen Mankind was shown for the depravity it was. God had then a seemingly impossible task on his hands: to put down evil with finality and yet uphold the gift of freewill. It was a task beyond the minds and means of all powers and authorities that had been created.

Then I saw in the right hand of him who sat on the throne a scroll with writing on both sides and sealed with seven seals. And I saw a mighty angel proclaiming in a loud voice, "Who is worthy to break the seals and open the scroll?" But no one in heaven or on earth or under the earth could open the scroll or even look inside it. I wept and wept because no one was found who was worthy to open the scroll or look inside. Then one of the elders said to me, "Do not weep! See, the Lion of the tribe of Judah, the Root of David, has triumphed. He is able to open the scroll and its seven seals."

— REVELATION 5:1-5 NIV

> I do speak with words of wisdom, but not the kind of wisdom that belongs to this world or to the rulers of this world, who are soon forgotten. No, the wisdom we speak of is the mystery of God—his plan that was previously hidden, even though he made it for our ultimate glory before the world began. But the rulers of this world have not understood it; if they had, they would not have crucified our glorious Lord. That is what the Scriptures mean when they say,
>
>> "No eye has seen, no ear has heard,
>> and no mind has imagined
>> what God has prepared
>> for those who love him."
>
> — 1 CORINTHIANS 2:6-9 NLT

The Son would be the fulcrum and the pivot on which the fate of Mankind would turn. But to put God's plan into effect required the Son to lay down everything. It was a journey from which there would be no return.

Forfeiting his omnipresence, laying down his omnipotence and shedding his royal radiance to be naked like Mankind, the Son humbled himself and was born into the human race.

> In your relationships with one another, have the same mindset as Christ Jesus: Who, being in very nature God, did not consider equality with God something to be used to his own advantage;
>> rather, he made himself nothing
>> by taking the very nature of a servant,
>> being made in human likeness.

> And being found in appearance as a man,
> he humbled himself
> by becoming obedient to death—
> even death on a cross!

— PHILIPPIANS 2:5-8 NIV

It was here in the dust of earth, the Son was born in blood by a fallen and spirit-dead human, Mary. Together with her betrothed husband, they gave him the name Jesus, son of Joseph. He was born into the family line of King David. He was born of the promise of God.

> For to us a child is born,
>   to us a son is given,
>   and the government will be on his shoulders.
>   And he will be called
>   Wonderful Counselor, Mighty God,
>   Everlasting Father, Prince of Peace.
>   Of the greatness of his government
>   and peace
>   there will be no end.
>   He will reign on David's throne
>   and over his kingdom,
>   establishing and upholding it
>   with justice and righteousness
>   from that time on and forever.
>   The zeal of the Lord Almighty
>   will accomplish this.

— ISAIAH 9:6-7 NIV

For God, the Son was now more than his first born, he

was to become the first born among the dead. His Son, now named Jesus the Christ, was the beginning and the pathway to resurrection for mankind. From this small beginning, through him, every vestige of evil would be destroyed. Through him all things would be reconciled to God.

> And he is the head of the body, the church; he is the beginning and the firstborn from among the dead, so that in everything he might have the supremacy. For God was pleased to have all his fullness dwell in him, and through him to reconcile to himself all things, whether things on earth or things in heaven, by making peace through his blood, shed on the cross.
>
> — COLOSSIANS 1:18-20 NIV

And so the task for which he was born began.

Here, in the dust, the Son of God now called Jesus Christ, began to deal with the rebellion within Mankind from the inside, learning obedience to God as a part of dead Mankind in a mortal body.

> During the days of Jesus' life on earth, he offered up prayers and petitions with fervent cries and tears to the one who could save him from death, and he was heard because of his reverent submission. Son though he was, he learned obedience from what he suffered and, once made perfect, he became the source of eternal salvation for all who obey him and was designated by God to be high priest in the order of Melchizedek.

— HEBREWS 5:7-10 NIV

This pathway, the journey Jesus Christ undertook, was shocking to the core. Even being foretold and forewarned, all heaven and earth were transfixed as he put his life into the jaws of the devil.

> Who has believed our message?
>   To whom has Yahweh's arm been revealed?
>   For he grew up before him as a tender plant,
>   and as a root out of dry ground.
>   He has no good looks or majesty.
>   When we see him,
>   there is no beauty that we should desire him.
>   He was despised
>   and rejected by men,
>   a man of suffering
>   and acquainted with disease.
>   He was despised
>   as one from whom men hide their face;
>   and we didn't respect him.
>   Surely he has borne our sickness
>   and carried our suffering;
>   yet we considered him plagued,
>   struck by God, and afflicted.
>   But he was pierced for our transgressions.
>   He was crushed for our iniquities.
>   The punishment that brought our peace
>   was on him;
>   and by his wounds we are healed.
>   All we like sheep have gone astray.
>   Everyone has turned to his own way;
>   and Yahweh has laid on him

the iniquity of us all.

— ISAIAH 53:1-6 WEB

Jesus Christ held no expectation that Mankind at large would recognize him for who he was. Even when given permission by the Father to give sight to the blind and raise the dead, he knew their condition for what it was.

> Jesus continued, "You are from below; I am from above. You belong to this world; I do not. That is why I said that you will die in your sins; for unless you believe that I am who I claim to be, you will die in your sins."

— JOHN 8:23-24 NIV

Clothed in dusty meekness and drab humility, a cloak contemptible for his rank, he was unrecognizable as the Lord of Glory. Penniless and poor, he walked a path unfamiliar to all others great and powerful before him. A path towards baptism into the depths of death itself. It was here in the dust that the once ultimate Son subjected himself to the ultimate shame: naked crucifixion at the hands of God's own beloved - Mankind - people willingly giving themselves over as puppets to the murderous wishes of the devil.

> From that time on Jesus began to explain to his disciples that he must go to Jerusalem and suffer many things at the hands of the elders, the chief priests and the teachers of the law, and that he must be killed and on the third day be raised to life.

— MATTHEW 16:21 NIV

"I have come to bring fire on the earth, and how I wish it were already kindled! But I have a baptism to undergo, and what constraint I am under until it is completed!

— LUKE 12:49-50 NIV

See, my servant will act wisely;
    he will be raised
    and lifted up and highly exalted.
    Just as there were many
    who were appalled at him—
    his appearance was so disfigured
    beyond that of any human being
    and his form marred
    beyond human likeness—
    so he will sprinkle many nations,
    and kings will shut their mouths
    because of him.

— ISAIAH 52:13-15 NIV

"As Moses lifted up the serpent in the wilderness, even so must the Son of Man be lifted up, that whoever believes in him should not perish, but have eternal life. For God so loved the world, that he gave his one and only Son, that whoever believes in him should not perish, but have eternal life.

For God didn't send his Son into the world

to judge the world, but that the world should be saved through him. He who believes in him is not judged. He who doesn't believe has been judged already, because he has not believed in the name of the one and only Son of God.

This is the judgment, that the light has come into the world, and men loved the darkness rather than the light; for their works were evil. For everyone who does evil hates the light, and doesn't come to the light, lest his works would be exposed. But he who does the truth comes to the light, that his works may be revealed, that they have been done in God."

— JOHN 3:14-21 WEB

And so as prophesied, Jesus the Christ was crucified. He walked into the executioners' hands. He was flogged and flailed, the skin ripped from his back and legs. Beaten and battered, he was nailed to a wooden beam and hung till dead.

It was the devil's finest hour.

Raucous shouting of celebration surely rocked the foundations of hell itself. The devil, the self-proclaimed god of the fallen empire, had cast down his foe.

But now, what to do with this man Jesus in shackles before them? It must have been here, in the heart of the devil-god's kingdom, their fatal mistake was discovered. To the horror of those assigned to bind him, no chain would remain in place, no yoke would hold him down. The Law of God, upon which such restraints draw their power, would not hold the innocent. Springing to life in their place were dormant words, words spoken by God of resurrection since the fall of man, now activated and alive by the sacrifice of Christ. The power of God pierced the darkness, and the Spirit found Jesus in the depths. A once impenetrable fortress, death itself crumbled around him, and amidst the screams of the demon guards, the captive within walked free. Jesus, now returning to his mortal body, passed right through the gates of Hades. Upon his passing they turned to ash, like a spider's web in the face of an inferno; from this point on even the weakest prisoner will walk through them as if they are not even there.

These were the very same gates that for almost the entire Second Age, had held the spirit-dead as *dead*. Jesus Christ was resurrected. Jesus Christ was now the First Born among the dead.

> But God raised him from the dead, freeing him from the agony of death, because it was impossible for death to keep its hold on him.
>
> — ACTS 2:24 NIV

> "Death is swallowed up in victory.
>
> O death, where is your victory?
>   O death, where is your sting?"
>
> For sin is the sting that results in death, and the law gives sin its power. But thank God! He gives us victory over sin and death through our Lord Jesus Christ.
>
> — 1 CORINTHIANS 15:54-57 NLT

The devil had been played. Jesus Christ, the Son of God,

even though now no longer omnipresent and forever bound to his human body, was made supreme in every way. He had become God's perfect Son, the key to enacting God's plan for the eradication of evil and the reconciliation of all things.

> He canceled the record of the charges against us and took it away by nailing it to the cross. In this way, he disarmed the spiritual rulers and authorities. He shamed them publicly by his victory over them on the cross.
>
> — COLOSSIANS 2:14 NLT

> Therefore God exalted him to the highest place
> and gave him the name
> that is above every name,
> that at the name of Jesus
> every knee should bow,
> in heaven and on earth and under the earth,
> and every tongue acknowledge
> that Jesus Christ is Lord,
> to the glory of God the Father.
>
> — PHILIPPIANS 2:9-11 NIV

Jesus Christ, now and forevermore of Mankind, was the head of all who would be resurrected. He would bring the rest of his Church, his Spiritkind brothers and sisters, to life through his death.

Spiritkind then is the race Jesus Christ brought to life. These are those who, through faith, cross from being dead to being alive. Through faith, they participate in his death and are granted resurrection - God's breath bringing their previously dead spirit to life. Though they still walk among those dead, they are separate from them: through Jesus Christ they are alive and continually being made alive.

> And he is the head of the body, the church; he is the beginning and the firstborn from among the dead, so that in everything he might have the supremacy.

> — COLOSSIANS 1:18 NIV

> Praise be to the God and Father of our Lord Jesus Christ! In his great mercy he has given us new birth into a living hope through the resurrection of Jesus Christ from the dead, and into an inheritance that can never perish, spoil or fade. This inheritance is kept in heaven for you, who through faith are shielded by God's power until the coming of the salvation that is ready to be revealed in the last time.

> — 1 PETER 1:3-5 NIV

Though Spiritkind and the spirit-dead still walk the earth side by side, they do not share the same destiny. Jesus Christ, the head of his Church, is perfecting Spiritkind, preparing them to rule alongside him in this age and the age to come.

> Then I saw a Lamb, looking as if it had been slain, standing at the center of the throne, encircled by the four living creatures and the elders.

> ..

> And they sang a new song, saying:
> "You are worthy to take the scroll
> and to open its seals,

because you were slain,
and with your blood you purchased for God
persons from every tribe and language
and people and nation.
You have made them to be a kingdom
and priests to serve our God,
and they will reign on the earth."

— REVELATION 4:6 & 9-10 NIV

JESUS CHRIST, HIS CHURCH,
AND THE END OF THE AGE

Now, as you read this, the Lord of all, Jesus Christ, walks among his followers on earth. He walks among those he has saved and called, knowing them, loving them, and leading those who will be led. He is with Spiritkind, his Church.

> "Write this letter to the angel of the church in Ephesus.
>
> This is the message from the one who holds the seven stars in his right hand, the one who walks among the seven gold lampstands: "I [*Jesus Christ*] know all the things you do. I have seen your hard work and your patient endurance. I know you don't tolerate evil people. You have examined the claims of those who say they are apostles but are not. You have discovered they are liars. You have patiently suffered for me without quitting."

— REVELATION 2:1-3 NLT

With great joy all of heaven offers fidelity and allegiance to Jesus Christ. Among those who have not fallen, there are none that are not in submission to him. Jesus is again, more so now than he has ever been, the Commander of the Lord's Army.

> I [John] heard every creature in heaven and on earth and under the earth and in the sea. They sang:
>> "Blessing and honor and glory and power
>> belong to the one sitting on the throne
>> and to the Lamb forever and ever."
>
> — REVELATION 5:13 NLT

The angels in his service are in preparation for a time called the Harvest, a period that is both coming and in many respects has already begun. The angels are his workers, receiving their orders from him regarding both Spiritkind and spirit-dead. The Son ultimately presides over how to handle both the devil and those who persist in belonging to him.

> Jesus told them another parable: "The kingdom of heaven is like a man who sowed good seed in his field. But while everyone was sleeping, his enemy came and sowed weeds among the wheat, and went away. When the wheat sprouted and formed heads, then the weeds also appeared.
>
> "The owner's servants came to him and said, 'Sir, didn't you sow good seed in your field? Where then did the weeds come from?'
>
> "'An enemy did this,' he replied.

"The servants asked him, 'Do you want us to go and pull them up?'

"'No,' he answered, 'because while you are pulling the weeds, you may uproot the wheat with them. Let both grow together until the harvest. At that time I will tell the harvesters: First collect the weeds and tie them in bundles to be burned; then gather the wheat and bring it into my barn.'"

...

His disciples came to him and said, "Explain to us the parable of the weeds in the field."

He answered, "The one who sowed the good seed is the Son of Man. The field is the world, and the good seed stands for the people of the kingdom. The weeds are the people of the evil one, and the enemy who sows them is the devil. The harvest is the end of the age, and the harvesters are angels.

"As the weeds are pulled up and burned in the fire, so it will be at the end of the age. The Son of Man will send out his angels, and they will weed out of his kingdom everything that causes sin and all who do evil. They will throw them into the blazing furnace, where there will be weeping and gnashing of teeth. Then the righteous will shine like the sun in the kingdom of their Father. Whoever has ears, let them hear."

— MATTHEW 13:24-29 & 36-42 NIV

This period is by no means easy for Spiritkind; the Church of Jesus Christ finds itself in the flames of persecution at almost every turn. Those watching on from heaven likely hold their breath in horror as waves of flames wash back and forth across the people on the earth. But amidst the carnage and the terror, as they continue to watch, a handful of those among Spiritkind begin to shine. Piercing stabs of light from amidst the darkness, among Spiritkind are now those who radiate like the sun. A brilliant luminescence exceeding even that which Lucifer had at the first, radiating from each as Jesus Christ brings them to perfection through the flames.

And now, as the age approaches its closing moments, the manifold wisdom of God the Almighty and All-Glorious is evident to all.

> Then there will be a time of anguish greater than any since nations first came into existence. But at that time every one of your people whose name is written in the book will be rescued. Many of those whose bodies lie dead and buried will rise up, some to everlasting life and some to shame and everlasting disgrace. Those who are wise will shine as bright as the sky, and those who lead many to righteousness will shine like the stars forever.
>
> — DANIEL 12:1-3 NLT

> "To all who are victorious,
>   who obey me to the very end,
>   To them I will give authority
>   over all the nations.
>   They will rule the nations with an iron rod
>   and smash them like clay pots.
>   They will have the same authority
>   I received from my Father,

and I will also give them the morning star!"

— REVELATION 2:26-28 NLT

PART VIII
CALL TO ARMS

NOW TO THE FRONTLINE

❦

N ow we arrive at the most perilous juncture in this book. This is the point where *you* enter the story. This is the point where the consequence of the Son's sacrifice irreversibly intersects with your own life.

I am sorry if you didn't want it to be that way. I know I've now put you in a position where you must choose.

Up to this point, perhaps you've taken comfort in the fact that much of what I've told you is from my imagination, details that perhaps you feel I can't possibly substantiate. Perhaps you are right, what I provide is nothing more than a map sketched in the sand. But I hope by it, somewhat like a parable, you might grasp these realities as they play out before your very eyes in the days to come.

So now we leave this hypothetical universe and enter *your world*. I am no longer explaining somebody else's story - I'm speaking to you, personally, right where you are.

❝ He has saved us and called us to a holy life—not because of anything we have done but because of his own purpose and grace. This grace was given us in Christ Jesus before the beginning of time, but it has now been revealed through the appearing of our Savior, Christ Jesus, who has destroyed death and has brought life and immortality to light through the gospel.

— 2 TIMOTHY 1:9-10 NIV

If you have put your confidence in Jesus Christ, the Son of God, then through his death and resurrection, you have been made alive. And alive for a *purpose*! This truth – that you have been saved for a purpose – is of great consequence.

The final battle is unfolding before your very eyes, and you, right now, are being called to arms.

Every child of God can defeat the world, and our faith is what gives us this victory. No one can defeat the world without having faith in Jesus as the Son of God.

... everyone born of God overcomes the world. This is the victory that has overcome the world, even our faith. Who is it that overcomes the world? Only the one who believes that Jesus is the Son of God.

— 1 JOHN 5:4-5 CEV & NIV, RESPECTIVELY

You have been given life for such a time as this.

MESSENGERS OF INVASION

J esus sent out the twelve disciples in Matthew 10 with
both a message and a mandate.

"As you go, proclaim this message: 'The
kingdom of heaven has come near.' Heal the
sick, raise the dead, cleanse those who have
leprosy, drive out demons. Freely you have
received; freely give."

— MATTHEW 10:7 MSG

The disciples were sent to people under occupation.
Under the occupation of the Romans, but more so, under the
occupation of darkness.

Isaiah speaks to that time.

See, darkness covers the earth
and thick darkness is over the peoples,
but the Lord rises upon you
and his glory appears over you.

— ISAIAH 60:2 NIV

To those whom the disciples were sent, to the people covered in darkness, the message that a new kingdom was at hand was a message of salvation. But they were not the only ones who heard it. To the fallen it was a message of invasion.

To the fallen, the disciples' authority signaled the end of their tenure. To the people receiving the message, it was the evidence of the new kingdom come. It is a kingdom of power where the fallen are cast out, where the sick are healed and where the dead are raised. It is a kingdom where not even death itself has the final say.

> "Jesus called his twelve disciples to him and gave them authority to drive out impure spirits and to heal every disease and sickness ..."
>
> ...
>
> "Heal the sick, raise the dead, cleanse those who have leprosy, drive out demons."

— MATTHEW 10:1 & 7 NIV

Here is what I want you to understand.

"The kingdom of heaven is near" is a message of an invasion. It means that territory currently held by the kingdom of darkness *can be contested.* Not just with words, but with authority and power. Anything the darkness occupies can be seized.

John the Baptist, giant among men though he was, doubted. And in the very next chapter, after the disciples were sent out, he called into question if what was reported was really the kingdom. Should they rejoice, or should they save their expectations for a future time?

> John, meanwhile, had been locked up in prison. When he got wind of what Jesus was doing, he sent his own disciples to ask, "Are you the One we've been expecting, or are we still waiting?"
>
> Jesus told them, "Go back and tell John what's going on:
>
> The blind see,
> The lame walk,
> Lepers are cleansed,
> The deaf hear,
> The dead are raised,
> The wretched of the earth
> learn that God is on their side.
>
> "Is this what you were expecting? Then count yourselves most blessed!"
>
> — MATTHEW 11:2-6 MSG

Realign your expectations and get clear on this point - the Kingdom comes from within, not so much from above.

When we look to see God's kingdom come, there is a tendency to look to the sky and hope to see God himself arrive, the power of God somehow to descend from heaven and transform the earth. In this scene, as it plays out in our heads, we are by and large a spectator.

But that's not how it happens.

To see God's kingdom come, we have to understand where his kingdom comes from.

> "Don't think you have to put on a fund-raising campaign before you start. You don't need a lot of equipment. You are the equipment, and all you need to keep that going is three meals a day. Travel light."

— MATTHEW 10:9-10 MSG

We are the vessel through whom God's kingdom comes. *You are the equipment.* It does not come from the sky; it comes from within us, his followers, his disciples.

There is one brief moment where the Kingdom did appear to come from the sky - Pentecost. A wind from above brought the Spirit upon each of the disciples. But then, for the rest of their lives on earth, the power for Kingdom occupation came from within. Even on that same Pentecost day, the words Peter spoke came from within *him*. Inside Spiritkind is where to look for the Kingdom of God.

> 'In the last days,' God says,
> 'I will pour out my Spirit upon all people.
> Your sons and daughters will prophesy.
> Your young men will see visions,
> and your old men will dream dreams.
> In those days I will pour out my Spirit
> even on my servants—
> men and women alike—
> and they will prophesy.

— ACTS 2:17-18 NLT

The Kingdom of Heaven advanced wherever they were. They were the vessels through which the Kingdom of Heaven came.

It is not an abstract concept. Hold out your arms and swing around on the spot. If you are full of the Holy Spirit, anything in that area is under the power and authority of the new Kingdom, the Kingdom of God. In that area, should you demand it in the name of Jesus Christ, darkness has to yield.

> People brought the sick into the streets and laid them on beds and mats so that at least Peter's shadow might fall on some of them as he passed by. Crowds gathered also from the towns around Jerusalem, bringing their sick and those tormented by impure spirits, and all of them were healed.
>
> — ACTS 5:15-16 NIV

It was evident enough to those desperate for God's touch that the Kingdom of Heaven, the place where darkness could no longer maintain its grip, was close to Peter. In his presence.

The Kingdom of Heaven was in the apostles. They were the equipment. And nothing has changed. You, the Spiritkind among you, are the equipment. The Kingdom of God comes through you.

> "Look, I am sending you out as sheep among wolves. So be as shrewd as snakes and harmless as doves. But beware! For you will be handed over to the courts and will be flogged with whips in the synagogues. You will stand trial before governors and kings because you are my followers. But this will be your opportunity to tell the rulers and other unbelievers about me. When you are arrested, don't worry about how to respond or what to say. God will give you the right words at the right time. For it is not you who will be speaking—it will be the Spirit of your Father speaking through you."
>
> — MATTHEW 10:16-20 NLT

It turns out that the people Spiritkind are sent to reach are as much a part of the kingdom of darkness as they are prisoners of it. Rightly so, Jesus predicts that people's response to this message is not always going to be with open arms. Many communities will turn on those declaring the good news.

> "When people realize it is the living God you are presenting and not some idol that makes them feel good, they are going to turn on you, even people in your own family. There is a great irony here: proclaiming so much love, experiencing so much hate! But don't quit. Don't cave in. It is all well worth it in the end."
>
> — MATTHEW 10:21-23 MSG

Among those who persecute Spiritkind are those God loves, lost sheep whom Jesus Christ is seeking to save.

For them, the kingdom of heaven is near, and through Jesus Christ there is no limit of power and authority for them to break free of all that has held them back in the past.

As Jesus said to John:

> "The blind see,
>   The lame walk,
>   Lepers are cleansed,
>   The deaf hear,
>   The dead are raised,
>   The wretched of the earth
>   learn that God is on their side."
>
> — LUKE 7:21-23 MSG

And that's the message, the message of invasion.

NIGHT IS COMING

> As long as it is day, we must do the works of him who sent me. Night is coming, when no one can work.
>
> — JOHN 9:4 NIV

The gospel message is a message of invasion, but it would be a grave miscalculation to think that the freedom it brings will be available forever. The clock is counting down. I tell you the truth, my stomach is in a knot as I type these words: night is coming. Listen carefully, these are not my words, but those of the Messiah, the Son of God himself.

Night is coming.

> For the Lord Himself will descend from heaven with a shout, with the voice of an archangel, and with the trumpet of God. And the dead in Christ will rise first. Then we who are alive *and* remain

shall be caught up together with them in the clouds to meet the Lord in the air.

— 1 THESSALONIANS 4:16-17 NKJV

Jesus is *returning!* And when he leaves for the second time, this time Spiritkind with him, the earth will be plunged into night. Christ will no longer be on earth in any form, and from that point on there will be only darkness. There will be no light, no salvation, no freedom, *for in the night that is coming nobody can work.*

> We must quickly carry out the tasks assigned us by the one who sent us. The night is coming, and then no one can work. But while I am here in the world, I [*Jesus*] am the light of the world."

— JOHN 9:4-5 NLT

Wake up. I mean right now. WAKE UP!

Shake the hell out of your bones and run. Fight the devil back with your bare knuckles and run from his deception, your life depends on it! Struggle free of the sin that entangles. In a dead sprint spare no effort to come to Jesus *now,* call to him, *now!* Call his name *now* while he may be found!

The night is coming, friend, like a wall of utter blackness, like a tidal wave of despair and anguish, it follows the split second after Christ's return. It has already crossed the horizon, the endless night of the end is almost here.

> Seek the Lord while He may be found,

Call upon Him while He is near.

— ISAIAH 55:6 NKJV

MARCHING ORDERS

❧

You are a messenger and a warrior of Kingdom invasion. And in these, the final hours of the last battle, you are being called to arms. These are your marching orders.

ONE. WAIT ON GOD UNTIL BEING SENT.

> He says, "Be still, and know that I am God; I will be exalted among the nations, I will be exalted in the earth."

— PSALM 46:10 NIV

Even Jesus, seeing the need for some *thirty years*, waited until authorized by God and empowered by the Holy Spirit before acting.

> As soon as Jesus was baptized, he went up out of
> the water. At that moment heaven was opened,
> and he saw the Spirit of God descending like a
> dove and alighting on him. And a voice from
> heaven said, "This is my Son, whom I love; with
> him I am well pleased."

— MATTHEW 3:16-17 NIV

Waiting is not without purpose. It was the last command of Christ to those who followed him. It is *in the waiting* that you learn how to make your home in him, and he his home in you.

> Those who live in the shelter of the Most High
>   will find rest in the shadow of the Almighty.

— PSALM 91:1 NLT

> ...he gave them this command: "Do not leave
> Jerusalem, but wait for the gift my Father
> promised, which you have heard me speak
> about. For John baptized with water, but in a
> few days you will be baptized with the Holy
> Spirit."

— ACTS 1:4-5 NIV

For some of you, this time of waiting will be laced with testing. From the least to the greatest, from the most accomplished and respected to the brand new among Spiritkind, resolve in your heart a fierce desire to stay the path. Let these hard times push you towards God, not from him, and you will be refined, purified and made perfect.

> Wise leaders will give instruction to many, but these teachers will die by fire and sword, or they will be jailed and robbed. During these persecutions, little help will arrive, and many who join them will not be sincere. And some of the wise will fall victim to persecution. In this way, they will be refined and cleansed and made pure until the time of the end…

— DANIEL 11:33-35 NLT

> Those who are wise will shine as bright as the sky, and those who lead many to righteousness will shine like the stars forever.

— DANIEL 12:3 NLT

> I have refined you, but not as silver is refined.
>   Rather, I have refined you
>   in the furnace of suffering.
>   I will rescue you for my sake—
>   yes, for my own sake!
>   I will not let my reputation be tarnished

— ISAIAH 48:10-11 NLT

TWO. PRAY FOR THE KINGDOM OF GOD TO COME.

The foremost thing to pray for - as instructed by Jesus Christ himself – is that the Kingdom of God should come.

> "This, then, is how you should pray:
>   'Our Father in heaven,
>   hallowed be your name,
>   your kingdom come,
>   your will be done,
>   on earth as it is in heaven.'"

— MATTHEW 6:9-10 NIV

Jesus never expected you to do it alone. He himself is praying with you. *'Our Father'* is a collective phrase used by two people praying to the one Father. Start here, you and Christ together, and pray to your collective Father. Learn to pray together with the Spirit of Jesus Christ.

> Pray in the Spirit at all times and on every occasion.

— EPHESIANS 6:18 NLT

THREE. SUIT UP.

Get into the armor that has been set apart for you. No soldier wants to find himself on the frontline without his clothing, protection, and weapons. Spare no effort. Make every hour count.

> Therefore put on the whole armor of God, that you may be able to withstand in the evil day, and having done all, to stand. Stand therefore, having the utility belt of truth buckled around your waist, and having put on the breastplate of

righteousness, and having fitted your feet with the preparation of the Good News of peace, above all, taking up the shield of faith, with which you will be able to quench all the fiery darts of the evil one.

— EPHESIANS 6:13-16 WEB

FOUR. EXPECTANTLY SEEK THE HOLY SPIRIT.

Waiting, at least in the first part, comes to an end with the arrival of the Holy Spirit. And with the Holy Spirit comes your commissioning. And in the same way that the Kingdom of God comes through Spiritkind, commissioning often comes through the laying on of hands of those who already have been commissioned.

> "...you will receive power when the Holy Spirit comes on you; and you will be my witnesses in Jerusalem, and in all Judea and Samaria, and to the ends of the earth."

— ACTS 1:8 NIV

> On the day of Pentecost all the believers were meeting together in one place. Suddenly, there was a sound from heaven like the roaring of a mighty windstorm, and it filled the house where they were sitting.

Then, what looked like flames or tongues of fire appeared and settled on each of them.

— ACTS 2:1-3 NLT

FIVE. NOW IS YOUR TIME.

Jesus said, "Peace be with you! As the Father has sent me, I am sending you." And with that he breathed on them and said, "Receive the Holy Spirit.

— JOHN 20:21-22 NIV

Receiving empowerment by the Holy Spirit confirms your commissioning. Your commissioning is confirmed by the power of God.

"These miraculous signs will accompany those who believe: They will cast out demons in my name, and they will speak in new languages. They will be able to handle snakes with safety, and if they drink anything poisonous, it won't hurt them. They will be able to place their hands on the sick, and they will be healed."

— MARK 16:17-18 NLT

You have been sent. So go!

PART IX
ANNEXURE 1

THE LANGUAGE OF LIES

L anguage is defined as the method of human
communication. Spoken or written, it consists
simply of words structured in a conventional way.

When the Son of God became Jesus Christ and dwelt
among us he spoke using our language. Using the same
words and structure, he spoke using the conventional
method of stringing a sentence together. Remarkably,
however, people were unable to hear him.

"Why is my language not clear to you?" Jesus said in John 8
(NIV).

What a great question.

If, when you read the bible, you have trouble making
sense of what has been written, then this could well be the
most important question to ask. Why, when Jesus speaks, is
what he says not clear? Why are we unable to hear?

It is a question of language.

We may well use the same words, but believe it or not, we
speak two entirely different languages. Our language, as it
turns out, for the most part goes undetected. It is a language
we know very little about.

VERSAL AND VERSION

❦

> "For this people's heart has become calloused; they hardly hear with their ears, and they have closed their eyes. Otherwise they might see with their eyes, hear with their ears, understand with their hearts and turn, and I would heal them."

— MATTHEW 13:15 NIV

Over ten times Jesus is recorded as saying to those who listened: *"Whoever has ears to hear, let them hear."*

Why on earth does he need to say this?

Jesus knew the truth. Jesus knew he was not speaking a language we are familiar with.

Although we are all using the same words, structured in a conventional way and understood by all, there are actually two languages being used. One is the language of truth, and the other is the language of lies.

In describing the Guardian Universe, I call the first Versal and the second Version. But here, I will refer to them simply as the language of truth and the language of lies.

How can lying possibly be a language? That is a great question, and in fact, it was the question that led me down this path in the first place. In John 8:44 Jesus says of the devil, *"When he lies, he speaks his native language"* (NIV). We're not talking about a conventional language, and different translations of this gospel render the phrase in a variety of different terms, such as *'lying nature,' 'resources,'* and *'character.'* But if a language, albeit one with unusual or unexpected characteristics, then things should come into alignment when we step back to assess this conclusion in context of the chapter, and indeed the whole bible. It's that journey that I want to share with you.

My starting point was John 8.

As it turns out, the conversation between Jesus and his believers recorded from John 8:31 is something of a showcase. At this moment in history, the language of lies is thrust into the limelight with its many unique, remarkable, and dangerous attributes on full display.

The first feature of this language is the reason it's able to be observed. Simply put, the language of lies obstructs those who practice it from participating in the second language, the language of truth.

This, of course, is a surprise, because those who practice lying believe that they are capable of both. Believing they can speak both, is also in an ironic twist, itself a lie.

How can this be the case?

It is best to go back to the beginning, to the origin and the source of it all, a passage of scripture that has been quoted numerous times in this book.

> "He [*the devil*] was a murderer from the beginning, not holding to the truth, for there is no

truth in him. When he lies, he speaks his native language, for he is a liar and the father of lies."

— JOHN 8:44 NIV

One thing we know for sure about the devil, Jesus credits him with the invention of the lie. Lying is his native language.

Which of course makes no sense. Your native language should be that which you spoke first. And the devil, being a fallen angel, should have spoken truth first.

But Jesus makes clear: he is both the father of the lie and a native speaker.

And so the first rule for this language becomes clear.

NATIVE TONGUE

R ule One. The language of lies will, with
commitment and practice, become your native
language.

I grew up speaking English and it's safe to say I'm not
aware of when I'm doing it. It just flows out of me. It is the
unconscious expression of who I am.

It is the same with those most profound at lying; they
speak deception without stopping to think. There is no self-
awareness. It has become their native language.

> To the Jews who had believed him, Jesus said, "If
> you hold to my teaching, you are really my disci-
> ples. Then you will know the truth, and the
> truth will set you free."
>
> They answered him, "We are Abraham's
> descendants and have never been slaves of
> anyone. How can you say that we shall be set
> free?"
>
> Jesus replied, "Very truly I tell you, everyone

who sins is a slave to sin. Now a slave has no permanent place in the family, but a son belongs to it forever. So if the Son sets you free, you will be free indeed. I know that you are Abraham's descendants. Yet you are looking for a way to kill me, because you have no room for my word. I am telling you what I have seen in the Father's presence, and you are doing what you have heard from your father."

"Abraham is our father," they answered.

"If you were Abraham's children," said Jesus, "then you would do what Abraham did. As it is, you are looking for a way to kill me, a man who has told you the truth that I heard from God. Abraham did not do such things. You are doing the works of your own father."

"We are not illegitimate children," they protested. "The only Father we have is God himself."

Jesus said to them, "If God were your Father, you would love me, for I have come here from God. I have not come on my own; God sent me. Why is my language not clear to you? Because you are unable to hear what I say. You belong to your father, the devil, and you want to carry out your father's desires. He was a murderer from the beginning, not holding to the truth, for there is no truth in him. When he lies, he speaks his native language, for he is a liar and the father of lies. Yet because I tell the truth, you do not believe me! Can any of you prove me guilty of sin? If I am telling the truth, why don't you believe me? Whoever belongs to God hears what

God says. The reason you do not hear is that you do not belong to God.

The Jews answered him, "Aren't we right in saying that you are a Samaritan and demon-possessed?"

"I am not possessed by a demon," said Jesus, "but I honor my Father and you dishonor me. I am not seeking glory for myself; but there is one who seeks it, and he is the judge. Very truly I tell you, whoever obeys my word will never see death."

At this they exclaimed, "Now we know that you are demon-possessed! Abraham died and so did the prophets, yet you say that whoever obeys your word will never taste death. Are you greater than our father Abraham? He died, and so did the prophets. Who do you think you are?"

Jesus replied, "If I glorify myself, my glory means nothing. My Father, whom you claim as your God, is the one who glorifies me. Though you do not know him, I know him. If I said I did not, I would be a liar like you, but I do know him and obey his word. Your father Abraham rejoiced at the thought of seeing my day; he saw it and was glad."

"You are not yet fifty years old," they said to him, "and you have seen Abraham!"

"Very truly I tell you," Jesus answered, "before Abraham was born, I am!" At this, they picked up stones to stone him, but Jesus hid himself, slipping away from the temple grounds.

— JOHN 8:31-59 NIV

This is a profound moment in recorded history.

And yet as profound as it is, it is a moment that is almost universally experienced by each of us. Face-to-face with the absolute truth, yet not able to see it.

Keep in mind, this is a conversation between Jesus and people who believed in him. These were his followers. It all starts when Jesus says, *"Everyone who sins is a slave to sin".*

If we tally up the scorecard between Jesus and his Jewish followers the results are illuminating.

His followers assert:

Verse 33 - *"We have never been slaves of anyone."* FALSE.

Verse 41 - *"We are not illegitimate children,"* FALSE.

Verse 41 - *"The only Father we have is God himself."* FALSE.

Verse 52 - *"We know that you are demon-possessed!"* FALSE.

Jesus asserts:

Verse 37 - *"You are looking for a way to kill me."* TRUE.

Verse 37 - *"You have no room for my word."* TRUE.

Verse 40 - *"You are looking for a way to kill me."* TRUE.

Verse 44 - *"You belong to your father, the devil, and you want to carry out your father's desires."* TRUE.

No external evidence is required to check the score – the listeners proved themselves liars and Jesus truthful by their own actions: at the end of the chapter they attempted to stone Jesus to death.

> At this, they picked up stones to stone him, but Jesus hid himself, slipping away from the temple grounds.
>
> — JOHN 8:59 NIV

These people were facing both the truth in word and the truth in person, and they had no idea. Yet that's not the crux of the story: Jesus drew attention to the fact that in the face of cold hard logic they were unable to hear *truth*. It bounced off them. It's a wonder that Jesus bothered trying.

But he did try, and here's why.

A SLIDING SCALE

Rule Two. The language of lies is learnt over time, bit by bit, lie by lie. The language of lies is practiced on a sliding scale.

At the outset, a person can choose whether or not to participate. They can choose their words wisely. Or they can experiment with fashioning falsehoods. But every lie is a rehearsal for the next. And although imperceptible, the further someone moves from the language of truth, the more slippery the slope becomes.

Most humans, most of the time, speak with a little bit of each language. In so far as they're aware of any lie on their lips, they believe that they're in control, fashioning it for the effect they desire. Humans think they are, and always will be, in command.

But this is far from the sinister reality of the situation.

The more well-practiced a person's command of the language of lies is, the less they can hear and understand the truth. Ultimately their new native language will take over not only their tongue, but their eyes and ears as well. They find themselves a creature only able to speak, see, and hear, deception.

> "Don't take this lightly. You don't want the prophet's sermon to describe you: Watch out, cynics; Look hard—watch your world fall to pieces. I'm doing something right before your eyes that you won't believe, though it's staring you in the face."

— ACTS 13:40-41 MSG

Why is this the case?

The answer is simple. Those who master the language of lies weave their words from a fabric of truth. Truth is the building block from which their lies are constructed.

A simple lie in its most elementary form is simply calling something that isn't as if it is. But as the person develops a grasp of the language they realise it becomes far more effective to use truth as a building block for the lie. The lie is more easily swallowed, easier to understand, easier to believe, easier to sell.

And here's the outcome in the long term. The person who masters the craft, using truth to construct a lie, can no longer see truth as truth. Slowly and surely it all becomes the fabric of their lie.

> "Yet because I tell the truth, you do not believe me! Can any of you prove me guilty of sin? If I am telling the truth, why don't you believe me?"

— JOHN 8:45-46 NIV

They do not believe Jesus because they're using truth to

furnish a different story. They're using the facts in front of them to paint a different picture.

> "Aren't we right in saying that you are a Samaritan and demon-possessed?"
>
> — JOHN 8:48 NIV

This was a lie - perfectly contradictory to the evidence at hand. But this lie had been put together using truth as its building blocks.

They saw Jesus' friendship with the outcast as evidence for his half-cast origins. Jesus' miracles where the work of demons. And Jesus' sinless nature a deception of the devil.

To these people, the truth was completely invisible. The truth, right in front of their face, had been twisted into sticky strands of their own web. They swallowed their own distortion.

And this leads us to the devastating situation that is Rule Three.

AN INVISIBLE LANGUAGE

R ule Three. The language of lies becomes invisible over time. To say it another way, those who practice the language gradually lose their ability to see their own deception. And it's not just their lies they can't see, but also truth. Both truth and lies become invisible. The speaker, as they speak, is being blinded.

> Truthful witness by a good person clears the air,
> but liars lay down a smoke screen of deceit.
>
> — PROVERBS 12:17 MSG

Once proficient in the language of lies, truth in any form is invisible. It can't be seen or heard. The ultimate outcome is the outcome described in John 8. Jesus points out a profound truth: those to whom he was speaking had murder in their hearts, and yet they could not see it. He spoke the shocking truth about something as near to them as their hand to their face, and yet they could not see it.

> "If you were Abraham's children," said Jesus, "then you would do what Abraham did. As it is, you are looking for a way to kill me, a man who has told you the truth that I heard from God. Abraham did not do such things. You are doing the works of your own father."
>
> ...
>
> "At this, they picked up stones to stone him, but Jesus hid himself, slipping away from the temple grounds.

— JOHN 8:39-41 & 59 NIV

A fish doesn't know it's wet.

They had no idea they were completely indoctrinated. But don't think for a minute this is where it ends. The sinister nature of this pathway is only just becoming clear. Indoctrination is just the start. Lineage is the finish.

LINEAGE

R ule Four. The language of lies has a lineage. The art of lying aligns a person, confirms their connection in fact, into a new blood line.

> … whoever pours out lies will not go free.

— PROVERBS 19:5 NIV

It is a well understood scenario, to be entrapped by evil, entangled in a bad situation. But the language of lies has a particularly disturbing power, in that it connects those who speak it into a foul family tree.

Not just any family tree, the godfather of this particular family is the devil himself, the father of lies, its origin and first native speaker.

> For their vine is of the vine of Sodom
>   And of the fields of Gomorrah;
>   Their grapes are grapes of gall,
>   Their clusters are bitter.

> Their wine is the poison of serpents,
> And the cruel venom of cobras.

— DEUTERONOMY 32:32-33 NKJV

Where does the transfusion into the corrupted bloodline start? It should come as no surprise - it begins with a seed. The process starts when a person believes a devil-planted lie.

> Jesus replied, "The Son of Man is the farmer who plants the good seed. The field is the world, and the good seed represents the people of the Kingdom. The weeds are the people who belong to the evil one. The enemy who planted the weeds among the wheat is the devil."

— MATTHEW 13:37-39 NLT

The process is exactly that which was explained in Chapter 36: *"Message Seeds and Thought Plants"*. Becoming a person who belongs to the devil begins simply by accepting and believing the seed he seeks to plant, believing his lie.

It is a remarkable feature of his language – believing it and speaking it has the power to transfer the person into the devil's family – that they become a weed who belongs to him. The language of lies forcibly takes captive, at the most fundamental level, those who practice deception.

This shocked to the core those who heard it the first time.

> "We are not illegitimate children," they protested. "The only Father we have is God himself."

Jesus said to them, "If God were your Father, you would love me, for I have come here from God. I have not come on my own; God sent me. Why is my language not clear to you? Because you are unable to hear what I say. You belong to your father, the devil, and you want to carry out your father's desires. He was a murderer from the beginning, not holding to the truth, for there is no truth in him. When he lies, he speaks his native language, for he is a liar and the father of lies."

— JOHN 8:41-44 NIV

The reality is, those who practice the language of lies are building a new lineage within themselves. They're on the pathway to discover they've become a son or daughter of a new father. And it's not a superficial connection. Finding themselves grafted into their new family tree starts deep inside their own heart.

SEPARATION OF THE HEART

R ule Five. The language of lies is both caused by, and completed in, the separation of heart from mouth.

> They take delight in lies.
> With their mouths they bless,
> but in their hearts they curse.

— PSALM 62:4 NIV

Severance of the spoken word from the heart is the essence of the problem. And it would be an easy fix if it wasn't for the fact we have desperately corrupted hearts. A dark heart has no wish to be exposed to the light of searing truth, being always partial to a soothing smoke screen of shiny words to cover its substantial shortcomings. But that is the choice, to be either exposed as sick or hide like a leper under a pretense of health.

> "What sorrow awaits you teachers of religious law and you Pharisees. Hypocrites! For you are like whitewashed tombs—beautiful on the outside but filled on the inside with dead people's bones and all sorts of impurity."
>
> — MATTHEW 23:27 NLT

Determining to hide the darkness beneath a facade of goodness is the devil's game, but it doesn't have to be yours.

There is an antidote.

THE ANTIDOTE

❦

I f you are fluent in the language of lies, you are blind to the truth. Put more simply, practicing the language of lies blinds you.

In John 8 this reality was profoundly evident. Jesus shines a light on their slavery, but they can't see it. Jesus shines a light on what is in their heart, but they don't grasp it. Jesus himself, the Truth personified, is standing before them and they have no idea who he is, even when he tells it to them straight.

They are completely blind.

And see the very beginning of the account - John 8 verse 31 - these are people recorded as being believers! So if you can believe in Jesus and still suffer such profound blindness, what is the antidote? Where can we find God's solution to this profound problem endemic across the human spectrum?

Immediately after John 8 is John 9, and in this account, John records Jesus taking a man born blind and giving him sight. Perhaps in this we see a metaphor for a generation born blind. Perhaps in this miracle we see God's plan to redeem a generation from the sticky web that is the language of lies, and to open the eyes of people illiterate to the language of truth.

THE FIRST STEP TO TRUTH

> Walking down the street, Jesus saw a man blind from birth.
>
> His disciples asked, "Rabbi, who sinned: this man or his parents, causing him to be born blind?"
>
> Jesus said, "You're asking the wrong question. You're looking for someone to blame. There is no such cause-effect here. Look instead for what God can do."

— JOHN 9:1-5 MSG

Let me, if you will, re-tool the disciples' question.

Whose fault is it that the whole world is caught up in the language of lies? Who sinned that this generation is so blind to the truth? Who is to blame that this man has never once seen so much as a ray of light, that his entire world is darkness?

Whose fault is it? Do we reprimand him, or do we reprimand his parents? Jesus' reply is clear.

> "You're asking the wrong question. You're looking for someone to blame. ... Look instead for what God can do."

Here is, then, the first step towards truth. Look for what God can do.

Analysis of your language, awareness of the language of lies is helpful, but it will not reveal the antidote. Gaining sight, becoming fluent in the language of truth, it comes from God and God alone. "Look for what God can do."

> The Lord sets prisoners free,
>   the Lord gives sight to the blind.

— PSALM 146:7-8 NIV

This was the mission, the ministry, and the purpose of Jesus Christ, as declared in his own words.

> "The Spirit of the Lord is on me,
>   because he has anointed me
>   to proclaim good news to the poor.
>   He has sent me to proclaim freedom
>   for the prisoners
>   and recovery of sight for the blind,
>   to set the oppressed free,
>   to proclaim the year of the Lord's favour."

— LUKE 4:18-19 NIV

Don't look for who to blame. Look to God for the fix. And in this we find the second step.

THE SECOND STEP TO TRUTH

❧

> "While I [*Jesus Christ*] am in the world, I am the light of the world."

— JOHN 9:5 NIV

The disciples were looking for the origin of the blindness; Jesus' response redirects our focus to our actions and the solution. If you want to find the truth you're going to need a light.

> Jesus said, "You're asking the wrong question. You're looking for someone to blame. There is no such cause-effect here. Look instead for what God can do. We need to be energetically at work for the One who sent me here, working while the sun shines. When night falls, the workday is over. For as long as I am in the world, there is plenty of light. I am the world's Light."

— JOHN 9:3-5 MSG

Jesus is the cure to blindness.

What we must understand, however, is that many who profess to be Christians are blind, even if they've not yet realized their condition.

How can that be?

Upon turning to Jesus, salvation comes with sight, and often in a flash. Spiritkind newly reborn see the world anew; not just their savior, but their situation becomes clear. But as the eventual state of many Christians attests, the gift of sight can be stolen. For those who knew Jesus but have become blind, their pathway into the darkness will have been gradual.

Over time, allowing Jesus to become absent in our thinking, snuffed out of conversations, extracted from our lives, we find ourselves in darkness.

And even as you read these words very real darkness is closing in. Without him, your internal compass to the truth no longer has a clear bearing.

It is not like you are immediately plunged into despair and depression. More likely, rather, there will be a cold grey morning somewhere in the hazy future when you awake to a new reality. Suddenly, your entrapment dawns on you. Caught in the world's web of lies and deception you realize your life has been woven into the fabric of religious and secular society, and it's nothing but darkness. Turning to the right and the left looking for the path you've lost, you realize the awful reality. You're once again blind.

But you are not the first. This was the experience of the man in John 9 cured of his blindness.

Read his story again, and perhaps you will notice a similarity to your own. This man has a powerful encounter with Jesus, and he is granted sight, the ability to see the truth for the first time. He has a remarkable conviction and clarity.

But, without Jesus, navigating the web of confusion that follows, leaves him lost at the end.

Like us all, he needs the light.

> He said this and then spit in the dust, made a clay paste with the saliva, rubbed the paste on the blind man's eyes, and said, "Go, wash at the Pool of Siloam" (Siloam means "Sent"). The man went and washed—and saw.
>
> Soon the town was buzzing. His relatives and those who year after year had seen him as a blind man begging were saying, "Why, isn't this the man we knew, who sat here and begged?"
>
> Others said, "It's him all right!"
>
> But others objected, "It's not the same man at all. It just looks like him."
>
> He said, "It's me, the very one."
>
> They said, "How did your eyes get opened?"
>
> "A man named Jesus made a paste and rubbed it on my eyes and told me, 'Go to Siloam and wash.' I did what he said. When I washed, I saw."
>
> "So where is he?"
>
> "I don't know."
>
> They marched the man to the Pharisees. This day when Jesus made the paste and healed his blindness was the Sabbath. The Pharisees grilled him again on how he had come to see. He said, "He put a clay paste on my eyes, and I washed, and now I see."
>
> Some of the Pharisees said, "Obviously, this man can't be from God. He doesn't keep the Sabbath."
>
> Others countered, "How can a bad man do

miraculous, God-revealing things like this?" There was a split in their ranks.

They came back at the blind man, "You're the expert. He opened your eyes. What do you say about him?"

He said, "He is a prophet."

The Jews didn't believe it, didn't believe the man was blind to begin with. So they called the parents of the man now bright-eyed with sight. They asked them, "Is this your son, the one you say was born blind? So how is it that he now sees?"

His parents said, "We know he is our son, and we know he was born blind. But we don't know how he came to see—haven't a clue about who opened his eyes. Why don't you ask him? He's a grown man and can speak for himself." (His parents were talking like this because they were intimidated by the Jewish leaders, who had already decided that anyone who took a stand that this was the Messiah would be kicked out of the meeting place. That's why his parents said, "Ask him. He's a grown man.")

They called the man back a second time—the man who had been blind—and told him, "Give credit to God. We know this man is an impostor."

He replied, "I know nothing about that one way or the other. But I know one thing for sure: I was blind . . . I now see."

They said, "What did he do to you? How did he open your eyes?"

"I've told you over and over and you haven't

listened. Why do you want to hear it again? Are you so eager to become his disciples?"

With that they jumped all over him. "You might be a disciple of that man, but we're disciples of Moses. We know for sure that God spoke to Moses, but we have no idea where this man even comes from."

The man replied, "This is amazing! You claim to know nothing about him, but the fact is, he opened my eyes! It's well known that God isn't at the beck and call of sinners, but listens carefully to anyone who lives in reverence and does his will. That someone opened the eyes of a man born blind has never been heard of—ever. If this man didn't come from God, he wouldn't be able to do anything."

They said, "You're nothing but dirt! How dare you take that tone with us!" Then they threw him out in the street.

Jesus heard that they had thrown him out, and went and found him. He asked him, "Do you believe in the Son of Man?"

The man said, "Point him out to me, sir, so that I can believe in him."

Jesus said, "You're looking right at him. Don't you recognize my voice?"

"Master, I believe," the man said, and worshipped him."

— JOHN 9:1-38 MSG

These last three lines are remarkable, and the most pertinent to us right now.

Even this man with a powerful conviction of the truth

ultimately found himself unsure which way to turn at the end of the day.

> "Point him out to me, sir, so that I can believe in him."

The simple fact is, to navigate a world where the language of lies is in full force, you need a light. And there is only one.

For this man, having been rejected by those claiming to represent God, he found himself in need of a light. In need of direction. In need of help.

And at this point, Jesus, the light of the world, found him. And in the light of Jesus' presence, the man found the truth.

The same is true for us.

Jesus is the light we need in order to see truth.

THE THIRD STEP TO TRUTH

esus is the Light, he is the Truth, and by his light lies
are shown for what they are. To find the truth, Jesus
is the beginning and the end of our pursuit.

Herein, however, lies what looks to be a paradox.
Jesus is claimed by many, and many who do what Jesus never
did. They hate, they harm, they slander, they murder. Are
these people also walking in the truth? Or has the truth of
Jesus been absorbed into the darkness that covers the world?

This is the exact situation our blind man encountered in
John 9. The Pharisees claim to serve God. Jesus claims to be
God, and on the evidence at hand, he is. Jesus, God incarnate,
is in their midst. But to the man born blind, he walks into the
argument of the age: whose god is God?

And here we have Step 3. The reality is, the Living God is
who the Living God is. We must determine the real from the
fake. The truth from the lie. There is a myriad of
counterfeits.

> Some of the Pharisees said, "Obviously, this man
> can't be from God. He doesn't keep the Sabbath."

> Others countered, "How can a bad man do miraculous, God-revealing things like this?" There was a split in their ranks.
>
> — JOHN 9:16 MSG

The truth of who God is, like all other truth, becomes the fabric from which the language of lies spins a narrative. You have to be aware that your own opinion of God could well become a web, albeit God-shaped, that in time you can't see through.

That is exactly the Pharisees' situation.

Over time their well-researched and thoroughly thought through concept of God became their actual god.

So, when God himself turned up, it became apparent their concept wasn't God after all. The situation is this: they have swallowed their own story. Their carefully woven narrative has them looking at it the wrong way and now they're having a very hard time seeing through their own web.

Your opinions are only your opinions. Do not let them become more than they should be.

How long since you looked for God's fingerprints in his work around you? When did you last seek silence in order to hear God's whispered words? How long since you spoke to God - not a mystical 'likely not there' god, but but to the one who actually *is* there? The one who is powerful, eternal and loves you completely.

Do you seek the living? Do you seek the real, or are you satisfied with the form? Comfortable to stick with theory?

The life pursuit of the Pharisee was to the perfectly described outline of God, the theory of him.

They sought the specific detail of what God meant, for example, when God said, *thou shall not work on the Sabbath.*

Over time, well-meaning rabbis had built up a definition of the rule. This rule, along with all the others, had become the Jews' framework through which God, his thinking, his nature, could be understood.

This works fine until you find yourself face to face with the real and living God. A living being rarely fits into a framework.

Jesus, just prior to healing the man born blind, had said to those following him:

> "My Father, whom you claim as your God, is the one who glorifies me [*Jesus Christ*]."
>
> — JOHN 8:58 NIV

To put this in other words: you claim to know God, but you can't see what he is doing. You claim God as your God, but you don't recognize the one he has sent.

Their pursuit was to the framework, not to the actual living God. For him to turn up was never expected: they didn't have an eye to see what he was doing, they didn't have a mind to perceive his glorification of Jesus. And so, the trajectory they'd selected for their lives was set. Even when the God they claimed as their own was in front of them they couldn't see him.

This isn't the story of all Jews.

> Now the Berean Jews were of more noble character than those in Thessalonica, for they received the message with great eagerness and examined the Scriptures every day to see if what Paul said was true. As a result, many of them believed, as did also a number of prominent Greek women and many Greek men.

— ACTS 17:11 NIV

If the Jews Jesus encountered in John 9 were of the same character as those encountered by Paul in Acts 17, then the story would have taken a different turn. Imagine if their posture was to pursue the living God. Imagine if their discipline was to investigate. They would have discovered God in their midst! They would have come face to face with their Creator.

And the same is true for us. The same is true for you.

If you're ready to seek the living truth, you'll find him.

This is the third step.

The living and alive Jesus is the light. The theory of God in and of itself, and if you stop there, is darkness.

> You will seek me and find me when you seek me with all your heart.
>
> — JEREMIAH 29:13 NIV

Don't settle for second best. Seek the real thing. Seek the light.

THE FINAL STEP TO TRUTH

> Then Jesus told him, "I entered this world to render judgment—to give sight to the blind and to show those who think they see that they are blind."
>
> Some Pharisees who were standing nearby heard him and asked, "Are you saying we're blind?"
>
> "If you were blind, you wouldn't be guilty," Jesus replied. "But you remain guilty because you claim you can see."
>
> — JOHN 9:39-41 NLT

The devil's language, and the corrupted bloodline that it spored within Mankind, brought rebellion to its zenith. The language of lies was sovereign. Until the arrival of Jesus Christ.

With the coming of the Kingdom of God, Jesus brought the language of lies' reign to an end. In his presence, the language of lies is forever disrobed and dethroned. In his presence, those who trust in the power of lies are shown to be blind to the truth and those blind are given the chance to see the truth for what it is.

> Jesus then said, "I came into the world to bring everything into the clear light of day, making all the distinctions clear, so that those who have never seen will see, and those who have made a great pretense of seeing will be exposed as blind."

> — JOHN 9:38 MSG

The Kingdom of God is a revolution of truth.

But it is not a revolution as you know it. Many would wield the truth as a blunt instrument, a means by which to bludgeon the blind and bring judgment to those in the dark.

Jesus is different - he is truth with grace.

For Jesus says the blind are not guilty. *"If you were really blind, you would be blameless"*. The blind are not condemned. There is no judgment for these.

For those whom the truth has been made clear, however, it is the day to decide.

Those who refuse to side with truth when the truth is shown have then chosen their side. They have thrown their lot in with the liar. They have selected their lineage to be of the devil, and at this point, they bind their fate to his.

> "Since you claim to see everything so well, you're accountable for every fault and failure."

> — JOHN 9:41 MSG

He is saying, you can't call the truth a lie, and claim lies to be the truth, without inheriting the judgment awaiting the Father of Lies.

Where do you find yourself?

Religion means nothing. Finding the truth means everything.

> "Night is coming, when no one can work. While I am in the world, I am the light of the world."
>
> — JOHN 9:4-5 NIV

Seek the light.

> From now on, think of it this way: Sin speaks a dead language that means nothing to you; God speaks your mother tongue, and you hang on every word. You are dead to sin and alive to God. That's what Jesus did.
>
> — ROMANS 6:11 MSG

COPYRIGHT